We Could Possibly Comment

IAN RICHARDSON

Remembered

We Could Possibly Comment

IAN RICHARDSON

Remembered

SHARON MAIL

Matador
5 Weir Road
Kibworth Beauchamp
Leicester LE8 0LQ, UK
Tel: (+44) 116 279 2299
Email: books@troubador.co.uk
Web: www.troubador.co.uk/matador

ISBN 978 1848761-841

A Cataloguing-in-Publication (CIP) catalogue record for this book is available from the British Library.

Front cover picture – Sam Farr/ *The Bath Chronicle*

Every effort has been made to trace the owners of copyright material used in this book. If any have been inadvertently overlooked the publishers will be happy to make suitable acknowledgement in subsequent editions.

Typeset in 11pt Book Antiqua by Troubador Publishing Ltd, Leicester, UK
Printed and bound in Great Britain by TJ international Ltd, Padstow, Cornwall

Matador is an imprint of Troubador Publishing Ltd

*This book is dedicated to Ian's memory
and to Maroussia*

Contents

Acknowledgements

This book wouldn't have been completed without the help and support of all the contributors and a great many other people. In particular, I'd like to thank Maroussia Richardson, and Brian Sibley, who did a wonderful job editing the book and provided tremendous support. I'd also like to thank Anne Gilhuly and Morag McPherson for proof reading and other editorial assistance.

My grateful thanks go to Margot Aked, Christine Andreas, Elizabeth Barber, Phil Barker, John Barton, *The Bath Chronicle*, Isla Blair, Brian Blessed, Lorraine Bonecki, Cindy Brome, Robert Chetwyn, Jacqueline Chnéour, Alan Cox, Charles Dance, Sam Dastor, Andrew Davies, David Stuart Davies, Desmond Davis, Margaret Thomson Davis, Dame Judi Dench, Michael Dobbs, Sam Farr, Cindy Lou Fiorina, Diane Fletcher, Stephen Gallagher, Nickolas Grace, Sir Peter Hall, Susannah Harker, Philip Hinchcliffe, Ann Hopping, Nicholas Hytner, Celia Imrie, John Irvin, Vadim Jean, Barbara Jefford, Alex Jennings, James Cellan Jones, Stacy Keach, Estelle Kohler, Eddie Mail, Sadie Mail, Suzanne Mail, Paul Marcus, John McDermott, Paul McGann, Sir Ian McKellen, Abigail McKern, Ian McNeice, Dame Helen Mirren, Brendan Nolan, James Norris, Roger Lloyd Pack, Louise Plaschkes, Jeremy Richardson, Ken Riddington, the late Terence Rigby, Clifford Rose, Ida Schuster, Paul Seed, John Sessions, Sir Donald Sinden, Meg Speirs, Juliet Stevenson, Patrick Stewart, Joan Street, Strathkelvin Writers, David Suchet, Janet Suzman, Clive Swift, Stuart Urban, David Weston, Susan Williamson, Maree Wilson, Pearl Wise and Joanne Woodward.

Illustrations

SECTION III

I would like to thank everyone who provided photographs for this book. My thanks go especially to Maroussia Richardson who supplied me with many of her photos – several of which were taken by her.

Introduction

Receiving the email from Maroussia Richardson just after nine on the morning of Friday 9 February, 2007, informing me that Ian had died peacefully in his sleep during the night, was one of the saddest moments I've experienced.

It had been one of my greatest joys and privileges to have become his friend. Getting to know Ian both as an actor and a person greatly enriched my life. His friendship and support through the years made an incalculable difference to me. His kindness and his giving nature touched me more than can be expressed in mere words.

Once the shock of his sudden and totally unexpected passing had lessened, I knew that I had to do something to honour his memory and to provide a testimony to what he meant to so many people. I am grateful to Maroussia for sanctioning a book in tribute to Ian.

Within the context of a look at his career, this book includes the tributes and memories of many of the actors, directors, writers, producers, crew and others who worked with Ian. I'm indebted to everyone who provided input - not only for their contributions, but also for their support and enthusiasm for the project.

As you will read, I am far from being alone in having my life enriched by a singularly special man, with a wonderful talent and dedication to his profession, and also with an enormous generosity of spirit.

I've also included the memories of admirers who derived so much pleasure from his performances and who became friends of his. I believe that the extent to which Ian appreciated those who supported him in his career was quite unique. He engaged in lengthy correspondence with fans throughout the world over the years and showed his appreciation of that support to a remarkable degree, as you will discover.

In addition to people's memories, there is an overview of his career, extracts from a lengthy interview I carried out with Ian in 2004 and some of my recollections of him.

The task is complete, but without Ian a huge gap remains in the lives of those who knew, loved and admired him.

Fortunately, he has left a wonderful legacy behind and a place in the hearts of so many.

Sharon Mail
Glasgow, March, 2009

Memories that will Remain Forever

The opening shot of the first episode was Ian as Urquhart, seated at his desk. The camera is behind him looking down over his shoulder, focused on what he is looking at – a framed photo of Mrs Thatcher. After a moment he puts the photo into a desk drawer, closes it, turns his face up towards us and says, "Nothing lasts forever. Even the longest, the most glittering reign must come to an end some day."
Then he coldly smiles. Wow!

Thus director Paul Seed describes the beginning of the BBC Drama series, *House of Cards*, and his reaction.

House of Cards, first broadcast in November 1990, catapulted Ian Richardson to stardom. His portrayal of Francis Urquhart, the ultra-suave Tory chief whip, who schemes and murders his way to power, was one of Television's most compelling performances.

Two further series, *To Play the King* and *The Final Cut*, were made, to great critical acclaim. Ian's depiction of the silkily scheming politician won him BAFTA, Broadcasting Press Guild and Royal Variety Club awards, several nominations and an army of admirers.

It was through Francis Urquhart that I came to know Ian. I was aware of him as an accomplished actor before then, but was captivated by his breathtaking performance as Francis Urquhart in *To Play the King* – the second of the *House of Cards* trilogy. In December 1993, I wrote to Ian, telling him that his inspirational acting (and Andrew Davies' brilliant adaptations of Michael Dobbs' novels) had prompted me to return to my first love, writing.

After exchanging letters, my daughter arranged for me to meet Ian on my birthday in Chichester, where he was appearing on stage, in August 1995. *The Miser* was his first stage play since 1981 and my initial experience of seeing him 'live' was an unforgettable one. His performance as Harpagon [the miser of the title] was full of energy, invention and superb comic timing. He simply lit up the stage.

Following the play, I waited at the stage door as had been pre-arranged and his wife, Maroussia, came to greet us first, followed a few minutes later by Ian himself. If it hadn't been for that glorious voice I might not have recognised him. Dressed in white short-sleeved shirt and trousers, with a moustache, and a panama hat hiding a head that had been shaved for his role, he looked very different from the man I'd seen on television. And he wasn't as tall as I'd expected because he always seemed to have a towering presence in everything I'd watched him in.

We had been chatting for a few minutes outside the stage door when a Festival Theatre executive interrupted us. After he left, Ian turned to me and said, "Pompous shit – I can't be bothered with people like that!" He had felt it more important to speak to me, than to a self-important bigwig.

The lasting impression I took away from that first encounter was of a man of overwhelming courtesy and kindness who, despite the great, booming, totally theatrical voice, was very down to earth.

It was to be the first of a great many encounters – all of them enriching experiences. One such meeting was on 7 April, 2002, when I attended a performance of John Barton's recital programme, *The Hollow Crown – The follies, foibles and faces of the Kings and Queens of England*, at the Yvonne Arnaud Theatre in Guildford on the eve of a tour of Australia and New Zealand.

The performers were Ian, Dame Diana Rigg, Sir Donald Sinden and Sir Derek Jacobi – referred to in one Australian newspaper as 'A Dame, Two Knights and a Commander.' Although made a Commander of the British Empire in 1989, Ian never received the knighthood he richly deserved and many people assumed he had been awarded. He was often referred to as 'Sir Ian Richardson' and indeed was accorded the title in the credits of one of the television dramas he starred in.

Spotting me in the street in Guildford before the performance, Ian and Maroussia ushered me in to the theatre to have tea with them, theatre director James Barber and producer Duncan Weldon.

In July, following the tour, there was a week's run of *The Hollow Crown* at the Shakespeare Memorial Theatre in Stratford, with Janet Suzman having replaced Diana Rigg. Throughout the years I'd told the Richardsons and my parents so much about each other and decided it was time they met. I drove the three of us down to Stratford and tried to invite Ian and Maroussia to lunch with us and an American friend, Ann Hopping. Typically, Maroussia had already booked for us to dine with them at their hotel, the Alveston Manor.

We had a rather special lunch. Ours was the only table occupied in the dining room and when it came to the main course our dishes were brought in complete with high-domed silver covers. Three members of staff positioned themselves around the table and lifted the lids simultaneously. Ian told us that his boiled egg had been delivered to his room that morning, covered by a similar contraption. It had been so well sealed in, however, that no amount of force by him could prise the lid off and a replacement egg had to be sent for.

Ian and Maroussia told us stories about the Antipodean tour, how they had been feted everywhere, stayed in luxury hotels and royally looked after by the tour manager, Frank Harlow.

After the show we waited near the stage door, wanting to tell Ian how much we'd enjoyed his performance. It was a pleasure to stand back and watch whilst he and the other actors patiently and courteously signed programmes, posed for photos and chatted to members of the audience. Ian was the last to finish signing and we went to say our goodbyes – or so we thought.

He insisted that he and Maroussia escort my parents back to our hotel and didn't require persuading when my mother invited him in for a 'wee dram'. During the course of a couple of drams, Ian held court. When he wasn't working, he liked to live his life as quietly as possible, but when he was in the midst of a theatre run or filming, he was at his most gregarious.

When he'd been filming in Ireland (he deferred to Maroussia to tell us the story, because her Irish accent was better) we were told that they had stopped on a country road to ask for directions. A couple of locals had come over to the car and said, "You don't want to be going this way – you'd better go that way." "And how far is it?" "Well," the locals had responded, "it's about four miles, but in your car it will be less."

Ian also spoke about a film that he was hoping to make with Charlotte Rampling in which he was to play her husband. He expressed his delight at working with such an attractive co-star, whilst instantly apologising to Maroussia for such an admission. That particular role never materialised but he did eventually get to play Charlotte's husband in a French film comedy, *Désaccord Parfait*, the penultimate film he was to make.

He was always the most entertaining and interesting raconteur, whether talking about meeting Indira Gandhi in India whilst playing her father, Jawaharlal Nehru, or recalling in graphic detail trying to treat a "serious illness" – haemorrhoids - whilst on an RSC tour of Japan; giving his feelings about the music of Schoenberg – "You'd be just as well listening to someone exploding wind down a lavatory;" or talking about the latest exploits of his grandchildren, whom he adored. As he told us in Stratford, asking him to talk was like turning on a tap – he would just keep going until someone turned him off.

By his own admission, discretion was not one of his finer points. He once told me that he had been interviewed for radio whilst in a play and had been asked which places it would be visiting on tour. Thinking his words would only be broadcast on local radio, he described one of the towns as 'Godforsaken' only to discover, to his horror, that his words were aired nationally.

In 2003, I took my parents down to Winchester for another recital jaunt. This time it was for a programme called *Fond and Familiar*, which Ian was performing with Dame Judi Dench and Bill Nighy. Judi was no stranger to F&F, but for both Ian and Bill it was the first time. Ian was particularly nervous, especially as there was going to be something unique about the occasion. It was the first time in a great number of years that Maroussia wasn't by his side to look after him. Instead, she was taking part in a reading of *The Epic of Gilgamesh*, with Prunella Scales, Timothy West and others, that afternoon in London. It meant that she wasn't able to join Ian in Winchester until after his recital had finished.

We had been told to make our way to the main theatre bar after the performance and trying to get there, found Ian sitting at a table signing autographs, with his usual charm and patience. When we managed to get him over to the bar for the pint 'with his name on it', he was in a great state of agitation, wondering why Maroussia still wasn't there. As soon as she arrived he rushed straight over and hugged her as if they had been reunited after a separation of some months rather than hours.

Ian made a point of bringing Judi Dench over to meet me and my parents and he, Judi and Maroussia were happy to pose for a photo. I only took the one, with my new digital camera and Ian said, "Are you sure you got it okay?" I checked the camera, nodded my head and let them get back to their drinks.

It transpired that we were staying in the same hotel as the Richardsons and we spent more time chatting with them and one or two others in the bar there. When I went up to my room, I discovered that I had two lovely photos of Bill Nighy but the one I'd taken of Ian, Judi and Maroussia was nowhere to be seen.

On arriving for breakfast the next morning, Ian and Maroussia were already tapping their boiled eggs. I thought I'd better 'fess up.'

"You know that lovely photo I took of you with Dame Judi last night?"

"Yes?"

"Well, it's not in the camera now."

I got the full Urquhart look. "For goodness sake, didn't you read the manual?"

This was immediately followed by, "Not to worry – I think someone took a few photos for the charity so I'll send you one."

I arranged to go down to visit Ian and Maroussia at the start of April, 2004, in their beautiful home, buried deep in the Devon countryside. There were two main reasons for the visit. I was going to interview Ian and also to deliver a present to him on what was the eve of his 70th birthday. Together with several friends, I'd managed to purchase a painting of Dartmoor that we thought he would like and I wanted to make sure it reached him safely.

I had intended to find a hotel in Exeter, but Maroussia offered to make a booking for me at The King's Arms in Tedburn St Mary, the village nearest to them. I flew down to Bristol, collected my hire car and drove to the inn. When I checked in I discovered that the bill had already been paid.

When I reached their idyllic converted cider farm (which I'd previously visited on a very foggy and wet summer's day three years before), they apologised for not having been able to put me up, due to the imminent arrival of their daughter-in-law and grandsons.

I spent three uniquely special days with Ian and Maroussia. The interview was a very focused but informal affair.

The rest of the time was spent relaxing and I couldn't have been made to feel any more at home.

I did, though, make Ian feel a little uncomfortable on a couple of occasions. One evening we went to a pub in another local village and I asked for a whisky and lemonade with ice. "Ice!" Ian, very much the Scot, reacted. "My father will be turning in his grave!" I've always had my whisky at room temperature since. I was also taken to a seaside town and we went into a pub for a bite of lunch. Fancying a lighter midday drink, I asked for a Malibu and pineapple juice. Ian looked at me and then stood at the bar muttering, "I can't believe I'm asking for this." I'd offended his masculinity.

On the Saturday, Ian took us into Exeter. He wanted to look at electric pianos – his 70th-birthday treat to himself – and shopping was needed. After the pianos had been looked at, food purchased and Ian had waited patiently outside a bookmakers whilst Maroussia and I went in, without a clue what we were doing, to place bets on the day's Grand National, we went to the Ship Inn, reputedly frequented by Sir Francis Drake.

Whilst there, Ian paid me the greatest and most touching of compliments by declaring that I was a soul mate. I can't think of a higher honour to have been accorded and I will carry the memory with me forever.

Back at the house, I spent a happy afternoon. Ian and I tackled a couple of crosswords (after he had 'chastised' me for using a biro rather than a pencil). It was just lovely to sit relaxing in Ian and Maroussia's company. Ian also did a practice reading of a speech he was going to be performing from *Measure for Measure* with Barbara Jefford later in the month, at a Gala Evening celebrating the centenary of John Gielgud's birth.

I remember too, that he had been given an alternative version of *Christmas Day in the Workhouse* (the original of which he had read very movingly at the *Fond and Familiar* recital). He read the adapted version to Maroussia and me – it was along the lines of:

> It was Christmas Day in the workhouse, the happiest time of year.
> The old men had their baccy, and the women had their beer,
> Up spake one young pauper, his face as bold as brass,
> "You can take your Christmas pudding and stick it up your ..."

Of course Ian never inserted the last word as he went through each verse, but by the time he had finished reading the poem we were all helpless with laughter.

I count myself so fortunate to have met Ian on a great many occasions and each meeting was a treasured one. I've also watched practically all of his film and television appearances and heard many of his audio recordings. He has left behind a wealth of material which I and others can go on enjoying.

For me, as for many other people, Ian Richardson really came into my life with *House of Cards*. But of course, he had already given a great many glorious performances over more than thirty years before Francis Urquhart burst onto our screens.

1

Swiftly Onwards and Upwards

Ian William Richardson, the eldest of three children, was born in Edinburgh on 7 April, 1934 to Margaret (née Drummond) and John Richardson. His father, a strict Presbyterian, worked as a manager at the McVitie and Price biscuit factory. Ian went to Balgreen Primary School and Tynecastle High School.

There was no theatrical background in Ian's family. Perhaps the only early indication of his profession came from the fact that his mother's neighbours noted that as a young boy, he used to get dressed up as a scaffie – a street sweeper – and go out with a brush and sweep the pavement.

At school he was 'a hopeless scholar', but his history teacher thought that he might have a hidden talent. Art was tried and rejected and then his mother arranged for him to have piano lessons. Ian became a competent pianist, but realised that he would never reach concert standard.

The big discovery came when Ian, just before his teens, was chosen to read Laurence Binyon's poem, *For the Fallen*, at the Armistice Day service. Instead of going to the lectern as was customary and reading the piece from there, he decided to stand at the front of the stage and recite it from heart. His history teacher told his mother that he 'was a born actor'. She arranged for him to have elocution lessons and he joined an amateur theatre company.

Ian had to do his National Service and most of his time,

served mainly in Libya, was spent as a Forces broadcaster. It was then, assisted by the chief announcer, and listening to his voice on tape, that he lost the Scottish accent that would, at that time, have hindered his career as an actor.

On being demobbed, he entered the College of Dramatic Art in Glasgow (now the Royal Scottish Academy of Music and Drama) whilst at the same time studying for a teaching degree at Glasgow University. His father was horrified at first at the thought of his son joining what he thought would be 'a band of queeries', but after he saw Ian's performance in *Lady Windermere's Fan* at the end of his first year, he pledged to support him.

Ian won the James Bridie Gold Medal at the College in 1957 and went straight to the Birmingham Repertory Company, having been watched by Bernard Hepton and selected to replace Albert Finney as the juvenile character.

He appeared in a variety of productions at the Rep, including a Christmas production, *The Enchanted Forest*, for which he wrote the music, and *The Importance of Being Earnest*. Critic Frank Dibb, commenting in *Plays and Players* in August 1959, said, "Ian Richardson gained further dramatic stature with his John Worthing and, again, I felt that I would like to see him in a Restoration comedy role. His Worthing had a delightful ease and precision."

His most notable role at the Rep was Hamlet, which he played at the tender age of 24.

In his book, *Five and Eighty Hamlets* (Hutchinson, 1987), the renowned critic J C Trewin commented, "In the mind, he remains 'young Hamlet'. During the spring of 1959, environed by the shades of so many actors before him, Richardson fought against his audiences' knotted and combined memories, and remarkably succeeded. In Hepton's production, keeping the play in an undistorted mirror, the dilemma of idealistic, baffled youth, Hamlet entered as a slight, sad-eyed figure of settled melancholy, a young man's single-minded sorrow. At that hour Richardson's personality had yet to develop. What would become a magnificent voice needed range, the larger theatrical passion, but the actor's earnestness and sweetness achieved much."

Brian Blessed – Actor

I was at Nottingham Rep and in 1959 I was seen by Barry Jackson [founder of the Birmingham Repertory Theatre] and invited to join his Rep. I popped over to Birmingham to see what it was like and there was a young actor in the Company, who was playing Hamlet. It was Ian.

I was absolutely enthralled by this young talent. He played the role with great vigour and purity. He didn't yet have the subtlety of experience, but the sheer energy and enjoyment and love of playing the part was so evident. It was vocally magnificent and full of variety and it was a wonderfully imaginative performance for such a young man.

I did join the Birmingham Rep and I remember Barry Jackson telling me once, that Ian was the most brilliant, compelling actor he'd ever worked with.

Onwards and Upwards to Stratford-Upon-Avon

Ian's stay at the Rep was brief, for in 1960 he was on his way to Stratford-upon-Avon and a stunning, lengthy career with the Royal Shakespeare Company. As Ian was to recall:

"I didn't expect the RSC to happen so quickly. My father was still rather protective of me. When I got the job with the Birmingham Rep, thinking that I was going to go south with all the Sassenachs [English people] etc., he decided to drive me down to Birmingham and help me look for digs.

We set off at about six o'clock from Edinburgh and the way my father drove, with no speed cameras or anything like that, we were in Birmingham by about nine-thirty and he said, 'You know, son, just down the road from here is the famous Stratford-Upon-Avon Theatre. Shall we not go down and have some breakfast?'

We drove to Stratford and went into this hotel just by the side of the river. I could see the theatre from the window at the table we were having breakfast at. I remember saying to my father, 'I promise you, Dad, I will play in that theatre before my time is up,' and he said, 'Oh, I'm sure you will, son.' Eighteen months later I was there. I just thought that it was going to be my Mecca – where I was aiming for. I didn't expect it to happen so quickly though."

One of the most important – if not *the* most important thing to happen to Ian – was that he met a young actress in the Company, Maroussia Frank, who was to be his rock over the years and provide inestimable support and stability throughout his career. Their first encounter wasn't one that set the heather on fire for either of them:

"In those days there were a whole group of supporting actors and actresses who didn't have a word to say, or maybe if they were lucky they got a sentence. They included Diana Rigg, Margaret Drabble, Roy Dotrice and Maroussia Frank, who was the daughter of a very brilliant theatre critic from the *News Chronicle* – a newspaper that is no longer in existence, alas. She and Diana and Margaret Drabble were walking on.

We were doing a production of *The Merchant of Venice*, with Peter O'Toole as Shylock, Dorothy Tutin as Portia and Denholm Elliott as Bassanio. I was the Prince of Arragon. In those days, you gave a reading of the play in character to your director.

It was my turn and I spoke with a certain kind of voice.

Michael Langham, the director, who was of Canadian origin, stopped me half way through and said, 'Can you lighten your voice?' I lightened it and he stopped me again and said, 'Can you lighten it even more?' I did so and he stopped me again and said, 'Can you lighten it even more?' and I said, 'You mean go into falsetto?' He said, 'No, Mr Richardson, what I mean is could you achieve an approximation of the tones used by our own dear Sovereign Lady?'

There was an awful chuckling all around me and I said, 'You want me to imitate the Queen?' 'In a word, yes.' I said, 'I'm sorry, I can't – I don't know how to do it.'

Michael addressed Diana, Maggie and Maroussia and said, 'Can any of you young ladies?' And this Kensington accent said, 'Well, actually, I can imitate the Queen quite well.' This beatnik, wearing filthy jeans, with long hair, unkempt and everything, sort of stood there and I looked at her and I thought, 'what have I been saddled with?' Anyway, Michael Langham said, 'After the read through you will take Mr Richardson on a boat on the river, he will pay and row and you will teach him how to do an imitation of the Queen.'

That's how Maroussia and I met and I quickly realised that she wasn't necessarily a beatnik and that the Kensington accent was genuine – that's the kind of background she came from. I fell in love with her."

Ian and Maroussia were married on 2 February, 1961 and their first child, Jeremy, was born in December that year, followed by Miles in July 1963. It was fortunate that one of the innovations at the RSC was the three-year contract. Being offered a contract gave Ian the security he needed to marry and raise a family.

Although he now sounded the complete Englishman, Ian felt very much at home having several of his countrymen in the Company:

"Other Scottish actors at the RSC at the time included Ian Bannen, John Laurie, whom I adored, Russell Hunter and Tom Fleming. I remember the opening scene of the famous *King Lear*, directed by Peter Brook, in which Paul Scofield played the greatest Lear ever. I was Edmund, the bastard son of the Duke of Gloucester, played by John Laurie and the Duke of Kent was played by Tom Fleming.

The opening scene is the Duke of Kent, the Duke of Gloucester and Edmund, and John Laurie had the first line, which he spoke with a very broad Scottish accent. Then up came Tom Fleming, influenced by the Scottish accent of John Laurie and up came I, trying to sound the same and it was the most Scottish opening to *King Lear* that you've ever heard. That was a great, great performance and it went on to greater things.

We took it to Europe in 1964 and were about the first Shakespearian company to go behind the Iron Curtain since the outbreak of the War. We went to Budapest, Bucharest, Prague, Warsaw, Moscow and Leningrad, as it was known then. I remember John Laurie standing up in the Stanislavski Conference Hall in Moscow and he said to the assembled company, 'All my colleagues have been reciting Shakespeare at you – I'm going to recite to you a wee bit of Rabbie Burns.' And there was an enormous cascade of applause because, you know, 'A man's a man for a' that', would mean very much to them. John began, 'My luve is like a red, red rose' and tears were pouring down my face. He did it so beautifully and they loved him for that.

On that tour we met Kosygin in Russia – it was about the time they were quietly plotting to get rid of Khrushchev [then the Soviet Premier, replaced by Kosygin in 1964]. Whilst I was in Moscow I was standing in a line trying to buy some caviar and Maroussia had taught me how to ask for things in Russian and I'd memorised it. But when they told me the price of it I burst into English and said, 'My God, it's much cheaper in Fortnum and Masons than it is here,' and a voice behind me said, 'Well it would be, wouldn't it!' I turned round and there was Kim Philby [one of the Cambridge Spies], which was quite an extraordinary thing.

Also on the tour, Marshall Tito [President of Yugoslavia from 1953 – 1980] came to a performance of *King Lear* I did there. He came backstage afterwards with his very attractive wife and we all shook hands. Of course it was extraordinary to think, in a way, of the privileges that come to an actor who belongs to a company like the RSC – the privileges of touring and being encountered by these famous people."

Amongst Ian's roles in his first few years at the RSC, were Arragon in *The Merchant of Venice*, Sir Andrew Aguecheek in *Twelfth Night*, Oberon in *A Midsummer Night's Dream* and Antipholus of Ephesus in *The Comedy of Errors*.

Sir Peter Hall – Director

The first time I saw Ian was in 1959. Armed with a contract, some savings and some hopes and supported by Peggy Ashcroft, I was starting the Royal Shakespeare Company. I'd heard that there was a wonderful young actor at the Birmingham Rep and went to see him, in *Gammer Gurton's Needle*.

What impressed me was his oboe voice – it was reedy with lots of colour in it. And Ian was also very fluent in his movement and found it very easy to time comedy. I thought he was ideal to join the young Company and grow up in it, which he did marvellously and very quickly became something of a role model to the younger actors.

He was very incisive and clear – it was obvious that he was saying what he was doing. He had a kind of tenacity about him both in comedy and tragedy and he was one of those actors it was impossible to ignore on stage. We thought of him as promotable material and that's what he proved to be. I think it was his Scottishness that made him so clear and incisive.

Speaking clearly in the theatre is part of the process of acting and it's got to be good. Ian had the extraordinary ability to parse a line of Shakespeare. He thought in lines, not in words and had a voice that carried and he could switch from pathos to irony in an instant.

The RCS's style was text, text and text and thanks to John Barton and the other people who were with me, we bred a generation of actors who could *speak,* and in the absolute forefront of that, was Ian.

He was always very engaging and very funny and I was extremely fond of him. But he was also quite emotional, turbulent and vulnerable. He took offence easily and was very easily hurt. He owed an enormous amount to Maroussia who kept him stable and clear and he was her life's work.

He worked with all of the directors. Directing Ian, you had to watch it and thinking on your feet had to be pretty brilliant.

I think one of the things that many actors have is complete anxiety about whether they are going to find the characters they are trying to act and he could be very moody, but I think he learnt to control and pace himself very well. And he was a great beneficiary of the company system as a young actor. He felt very secure at Stratford.

I loved his Oberon because he had such clarity of diction and lyricism and yet he was so devilish. Oberon does play the most awful trick on Titania and that devilish quality, which is really dangerous, I think he did wonderfully. He was excellent in *Marat/Sade* and *Coriolanus* and his Ford was a great comic performance.

For 15 years he was unquestionably one of *the* classical actors and played more than 30 parts at the RSC and that was one half of his career. The other half was in television, film and commercial theatre and he had a really luminous time in both halves.

The cost to Ian was great. He suffered terribly before going on stage to perform – I saw it for myself – and was very often physically sick. I think it wasn't until the '70's that he got to a point where he loved acting without paying any attention or suffering any misery. He was extremely helpful, particularly with the young actors especially as he became a senior citizen of the Company and I think he became more generous the older he got.

Ian gave us hours and hours of pleasure and of credibility.

—◆◆—

Clifford Rose – Actor

I was a founder member of the RSC along with Ian. He was wonderful as the Prince of Arragon and it was very unusual in that production, because of course Arragon had a rather aged mother and Maroussia played her – like this very severe Spanish matriarch figure and Ian had to be very careful what he said in front of her and it worked particularly well.

Later on in the season, because somebody was unable to play Sir Andrew Aguecheek in *Twelfth Night,* Ian, who was not contracted to do so, was asked to play him. Peter Hall felt this was a bit unfair on me so he said, "Why don't you go on as Arragon for some of the run?" I did, with Maroussia as my mother and of course I copied Ian's performance to the letter, which got me a lot of laughs.

The Comedy of Errors was a very simple production and a huge hit. It had many changes of cast and I wasn't in it at the start, but when it went on an Eastern European tour I played the Dromio of Ephesus to Ian's Antipholus. He was an extremely inventive actor and a delight to work with.

Ian also played in *The Merry Wives of Windsor* and although it wasn't a great production, I thought his Frank Ford was absolutely stunning.

We were both in the touring production of *King Lear* in 1964 – I played Albany. We toured all over Eastern Europe and then went to New York.

We then did the *Marat/Sade*, in which I played the asylum director, Coulmier. Ian played the Herald originally and he was fantastic. The next season, we played at the Aldwych and Ian took over from Clive Revill as Marat and Michael Williams played the Herald. We performed it in New York and Ian being the first actor to appear naked on the Broadway stage was quite an extraordinary happening at the time.

He appeared on the Johnny Carson show over there and he was really up to it. I remember watching it on television and he was extremely good and I thought that he wasn't just an actor but a personality who blossomed on interview.

We then made the film of *Marat/Sade* and Ian and I used to be made up at the same unearthly time in the mornings, sitting next to each other.

I saw Ian in *The Hollow Crown* at Stratford in 2002 – I'd done that show myself on an American tour. They were all brilliant and absolutely at the top of their game. Ian was magnificent in it. He wasn't content just to say the words – he had to add in little bits of invention too, by way of illustration.

As an actor he was consummate. A lot of actors who are great at speaking are not so good at doing the physical stuff – Ian had both. He had the most incredible voice that sounded like a trumpet and yet he had this terrific physicality and was also marvellous at comedy, which I think was a most unusual combination.

He made the transition to television extremely well. Again, a lot of actors who are great in theatre aren't so good in television, or vice versa. Not so with Ian. He really knew how to play for the camera, had enormous energy which you don't often see on television and could carry a drama so effortlessly.

John Barton – Director

I probably did more with Ian than anyone over the years. I first saw him playing *Hamlet* at the Birmingham Rep before he joined the RSC. *Richard III* was one of the last things he did in Stratford. I worked with him on about ten productions.

His voice, his technical skills, his emotion – you can't really separate all the different qualities because they were all part of him. Ian did *The Hollow Crown* first many years ago and it was a kind of spine for a lot of his work.

I worked with him from the beginning – even in plays he was in before I directed him. He was very intelligent but he was very much an actor – that's what he lived for and what he did. He became a leading actor early on and was highly thought of. He was one of the best I ever worked with.

He was very good, for instance, in *Coriolanus* in the fighting which he was very skilled at, like lots of things and he was apt to overdo it and had to control it. That happened with all actors. He was really bold and daring and he just knew every inch of the Stratford stage and could sense where he was. He was extremely adept at talking to and sharing with an audience too. He had it all really.

Unlike some actors, he didn't like people watching him rehearse because he knew he would start acting at acting and he felt that he was forcing himself.

I had to take on *The Tempest* for Trevor Nunn at two or three weeks' notice and I always thought Ian was too young to play Prospero, though he did very well and he should have done it again. He was probably the best Chorus in *Henry V* there has ever been.

He was a terrific comedian and could be very extreme in comedy, like he was as Ford and he was terrific as Bertram in *All's Well* – so funny. Although he had several comic roles, I don't think he ever had any of the great Shakespearian clown parts and I don't remember him ever pressing for these.

Richard II was based on the idea of the king being an actor and not really a king till later on. That very much appealed to Ian because he really was completely and utterly an actor's actor. He and Richard Pasco, with whom he shared the roles of Richard and Bolingbroke, loved working with each other.

The one thing I always wanted to do with him through the years and we never got round to it was the Duke in *Measure for Measure*. He played Angelo but I always thought the one huge Shakespearian role he was born to tackle – a mixture of all his qualities – could have been expressed in the Duke.

That was the role which nobody in England has ever really solved but he could have and would have, I think, because of the mix of a very contradictory part that was political, theatrical, ironic, tough and funny and goes two different ways. He was *the* person I thought could carry it off.

The last time I saw him was shortly before he died. He came to a workshop I was doing and we filmed him talking for about 10 minutes and he was bubbling then.

——————

Clive Swift – Actor

We both joined the RSC in 1960. I remember just creeping in at the back of a meeting at the Memorial Theatre with Philip Voss and Bill Wallis as the most junior of the juniors. Some of the most famous actors in the world were there. Peter Hall made his speech that he wanted to try and set up a company that would stay together for a minimum of three years and Peter O'Toole and Peggy Ashcroft had committed themselves to leading it. Peter (Hall) said it would be possible for members of all ranks to join.

Ian did his Prince of Arragon in *The Merchant of Venice*, with Maroussia as his mother. That was the first time I was aware of him. It was a wonderful performance because it was so inbred. The thing that

I most came to admire about him was his amazing diction and the clarity of his speaking and it was used par excellence as Arragon – almost in a half-voice, ultra sensitive and like a man who still had his mum behind him. It was a very effective performance. The audience loved it and he got many, many laughs.

The Comedy of Errors was a very whimsical, un-English production and was just delightful. Ian was brilliant as one of the Antipholus twins and that's when he first showed his real aptitude for farce. He also had a small part in The Taming of the Shrew – a huntsman figure. When it was revived, Ian took over Tranio and I took over Grumio.

Ian played Oberon in 1963 in A Midsummer Night's Dream on stage and later on in Peter Hall's filmed version of it. I was staggered by the fact that he could film all day and then perform on stage. I recall one day, when we filmed in the morning and then he did a matinee in All's Well and then Coriolanus in the evening. I remember thinking that was extraordinary as a feat of endurance.

When we performed Cymbeline I played Cloten, a very eccentric character, which was my best part to date. For once, I had a better part than him and he played one of my attendants. I remember Ian saying to me that I did too much as an actor – I should underplay a bit more – and it has always stuck with me.

The good thing about the ensemble company was that we could say things to one another and make suggestions. And the way Peter Hall had established the atmosphere, we could go and do that and all have our own input. We didn't realise how lucky we were.

In the permanent Company I wasn't aware of any real rivalries, which in itself was amazing. We were a genuine ensemble, and Ian was one of the stars of that. On the stage he was always cool, sometimes ice-cold, and he was more organised and in some ways more intelligent and relaxed than he was in real life. The stage was his absolute element. He was always in control on stage and was so effective in terms of an audience. He just knew that his timing and the way in which he said his words would bring the house down.

I used to fiddle about on the piano and I remember Ian writing music for something – I think it was *The King of the Golden River*. We both loved music, though he didn't play the piano in the rehearsal room as much as I did.

I saw him in *The Revenger's Tragedy*, which I wasn't in and wasn't familiar with. What I carried away from it was that Ian's speaking of it – the illumination of the text – was like a beam of light going down the page. I understood every word he said of this difficult, abstruse language. It's Ian who makes me remember the play and it was just totally outstanding.

His great virtue, certainly in the classics, was almost to stand back and present the text as in the author or the character's mind.

Dame Judi Dench – Actress

I first met Ian and Maroussia in the 1962 season at Stratford-upon-Avon when we were all in *Measure for Measure* directed by John Blatchley, and then *A Midsummer Night's Dream*, directed by Peter Hall. He was remarkable as Lucio and glorious as Oberon. His blessing of the house at the end of *The Dream* is something I will never forget and nor would anyone who had seen it.

Ian was a truly remarkable actor, a superb deliverer of Shakespeare's verse, totally at home in the theatre and with a wicked sense of humour.

When *The Dream* transferred to the Aldwych Theatre in London, my late husband Michael Williams took over the role of Puck. Part of the set was a huge tree in the middle of the stage and Ian and Michael set up a small bar inside it. There are large chunks of the play where Oberon (Ian) and Puck (Michael) do not appear and it was these times that they spent in the 'tree' in the 'bar'!

Ian and I did many recitals together. On every occasion, he was charming, wonderfully prepared and with that wonderful sense of fun. He and Maroussia were the most dear and loving friends. I never tired of hearing his voice, which was instantly recognisable and he was always eminently watchable on television. I could never imagine Ian growing old, but nor do I have to.

2

Rising to Prominence in the RSC

"He even, God forgive him, makes the art of the playwright seem redundant." So said critic, Hugh Leonard, writing in *Plays and Players* in February, 1965. The playwright was Shakespeare, the play *The Merry Wives of Windsor* and the actor who transcended the talents of the Bard was Ian Richardson, playing the insecure husband, Frank Ford.

The middle years of Ian's 15-year association with the Royal Shakespeare Company saw him perform a number of leading roles, including Bertram in *All's Well That Ends Well*, Vendice in *The Revenger's Tragedy*, the title role in *Coriolanus*, Prospero in *The Tempest* and Proteus in *The Two Gentlemen of Verona*.

Then there was that performance in *The Merry Wives of Windsor*. Ian played Ford in several productions during his time at the RSC. Reviewing the play at the Aldwych, Hugh Leonard further commented, "What the director has done for and to the play is of no account compared with what Ian Richardson does for and to the character of Ford. Mr Richardson's suburban husband is at first unremarkable: he even carries what looks suspiciously like a briefcase. But once he smells cuckoldry in the wind, a heady element of high drama enters Ford's life. He becomes drunk with the ingenuity of his own stratagems. But Ford is as inept an avenger as Falstaff is in the role of seducer. His moments of suavity are ruined by a squeaking shoe; when he flourishes a blunderbuss, it goes off like a demented cannon;

instead of merely ransacking a basket in search of Falstaff, he leaps, vanishes from sight for what seems like an hour, and reappears, murmuring apologetically; 'Well he's not here that I seek for.' Mr Richardson plucks laughs out of thin air; and, even without making allowances for the dullness of the character as written, this may well be the comedy performance of the year."

Sir Donald Sinden – Actor

I returned to Stratford in 1963 [having last played there in 1947]. We were doing *The Wars of the Roses* and also *The Comedy of Errors*. It was the first time I'd seen Ian act and he was incredibly funny as one of the Antipholus twins.

I'll never forget his fabulous performances as Ford in *The Merry Wives of Windsor*. I've never known such expertise with speaking and his erratic movement was wonderful. An actor is very lucky if he hits the part that he was born to play. Ian was born to play Ford and his performance was the definitive one.

Peter Brook's 1964 production of the *The Persecution and Assassination of Marat as Performed by the Inmates of the Asylum of Charenton under the Direction of the Marquis de Sade* was described by *Theatre World* as, "One of the most brilliant stage productions ever seen in London" and Ian's performance as the Herald as, "a brilliant portrayal of the abnormality of jaunty indifference."

When the production was taken to Broadway, Ian went as assistant director and was asked to play Marat, Michael Williams taking over as the Herald. Ian considered the Herald, who provides a narration throughout the play, to be the best part and much better than Marat. As Marat, he had to spend most of his time unhappily stuck in a bathtub and, being such a physical actor, it was a role for which Ian felt he was totally unsuited. The change of character, however, gave him a little bit of history when he became the first actor to bare his behind on stage in the States:

> "I would have to present my back to the audience as I got out of the bath. Across my front there was a clever little device which they couldn't see. It was made by someone in Soho and it was called a posing pouch. It was flesh-coloured and satin-lined, with a little label with the owner's telephone number on it.
>
> Every night when I came out of the bath there was this curious clicking noise. I asked Michael Williams if he could see what the noise was. He came into my dressing room and told me that many of the people in the audience wore glasses and the clicking noise was them raising their eyeglasses to see my bare bum."

Ian also played Malcolm in a production of *Macbeth*, with Paul Scofield and Vivien Merchant as Lord and Lady Macbeth and Sebastian Shaw as Duncan.

Peter Roberts, writing in the October 1967 edition of *Plays and Players* said, "Ian Richardson as Malcolm more than lives up to the rash predictions recently made for his future. He gains, of course, from the fact that the English scene is made the pivotal point of this production, which is at pains to establish a Christian view of monarchy and to point to the lack of any such Christian concept in Macbeth himself. Even so, Ian Richardson's verse-speaking is beautifully supple and his ability to present a 'nice' character who is not also 'wet' represents a welcome sign of versatility in his work."

Dame Helen Mirren – Actress

I think I couldn't have been luckier than to have started my professional career working with Ian. He was so wonderfully kind and supportive and unselfish. Not all actors were like that. A lot didn't understand or had forgotten what it's like at the beginning when you are so unsure of yourself. I was technically unprepared and hadn't even been to drama school and yet Ian was so unbelievably giving with his time, encouragement and ability.

We first worked together in *The Revenger's Tragedy* when I played Castiza, sister to Vendice, played by Ian.

I remember him best for his incredible technical abilities – that and the fact that he was the kindest man with the biggest of hearts. I think that communicated itself in his performances on stage. He gave very strong, charismatic performances on stage but he wasn't that kind of person in himself.

He had the most extraordinary voice – bell-like and with the most incredible internal power. And I just loved his comedic abilities. He was an absolute comic genius on stage and understood the importance of timing in comedy so well. He was amazing in his delivery of comic lines.

Ian was the most generous of men. I remember early on, I played a scene with him and he manoeuvred it so that I would get all the laughs I could get. And if I wasn't getting them he would teach me. Also, he would wait and make sure that I got my exit round of applause – something not all actors would do.

I don't know whether he suffered from nerves at all because he never communicated any nervousness in the rehearsal room. And he was never jealous or conceited.

Right from the beginning of my time at the RSC both Ian and Maroussia were incredibly kind and welcoming to me and to have had support like that made all the difference.

I never got the chance to work with Ian again after the RSC but it was always a joy when we would bump into each other over the years. And I'm just so very thankful that the last time I saw him, with Maroussia, two or three years ago, I got the chance to express directly to him my gratitude and explain just how much he had done for me.

At his Memorial Service it was so obvious how much he was loved by everyone. I think that was mainly because of his kindness and generosity – and it was a very simple and direct generosity.

———

Susan Williamson – Actress

Greatly admired by other actors who watched him hold the audience in the palm of his hand, his expressive voice which, with a whisper, could reach the back of any auditorium, Ian possessed a unique capacity for combining truth with a wonderful theatricality.

His Antipholus in *The Comedy of Errors* was wonderfully flamboyant and his comic timing brilliant. He was always 'spot on' in every performance – nothing phased him.

I played Simone Evrard in the *Marat/Sade*. Ian was a splendid Marat and took New York by storm. Theatregoers there had never quite seen anything like Peter Brook's production of the play and for months we were the toast of the town.

I remember that when we were in New York people who were unable to obtain tickets hid, in desperation, on stage. The slats of the baths in the bath house were raised and to our horror there were people crouching there. We had to get rid of them and Ian raised the volume of all of his speeches and banged his fists on the bath he was sitting in. I went to the side of the stage and told the stage management, who crept under the stage and got the protesting enthusiasts safely out of harm's way. Little did they know that they would have been jumped on at any minute. Ian was terrific – his huge and marvellous voice covering all the 'kerfuffle'.

Patrick Stewart – Actor

The first time I met Ian was at the start of rehearsals for *The Revenger's Tragedy*, which was directed by Trevor Nunn. When Trevor told me about the project he asked me if I knew the story and I told him I didn't. He said it was about two revenging brothers. He had asked Ian Richardson to play Vendice and he wanted me to play his brother Hippolito.

Although I hadn't worked with Ian, I had seen him act and knew his reputation and admired him immensely, so the thought that he and I were going to be playing brothers and be so close together was absolutely thrilling. What Trevor had omitted to tell me was that Vendice had about 90% of the lines. John Barton felt so sorry for me that he actually wrote me a soliloquy for the play.

What it did mean was that I spent weeks in a rehearsal room watching Ian and many hours on stage with him so I got, at close quarters, a master class in classical acting. In terms of clarity, specificity, enunciation – vocal fireworks, if you like – I had Ian as a wonderful mentor.

His whole manner and style in leading a company impressed me, too – the responsibility and the way in which one must lead from the front. Ian was marvellous at that and it's something I've come to enjoy myself.

I remember, during one of the previews for *The Revenger's Tragedy* we came to this big set change where a bed had to come on from upstage: we were all very nervous, not knowing how it was going to work. This was the bed upon which Vendice and Hippolito challenged their mother, played brilliantly by Patience Collier – it's a bit like the scene in *Hamlet* except there are two sons. The bed used to come down with Patience on it and we followed it. Well, it jammed and it wasn't going to move.

Ian, without any hesitation, moved quickly forward to the front of the stage and said, "Ladies and gentlemen, as you are probably aware we've had a technical difficulty with the bed. We do need the bed for the next scene in order for the play to continue." He made this wonderful impromptu speech – just like the flamboyant Vendice – and I stood at the back with my mouth open. I'd never seen an actor speak to the audience like that before. It was thrilling to see the confidence, the assurance and the articulacy of the man and of course the audience gave him a huge round of applause and when the bed was fixed and trundled down they gave us another. Ian would always leap to seize an opportunity like that.

I was in *Richard III* with Ian. I remember him as a precise and brilliant, technically virtuosic Buckingham. This was my first opportunity to hear him speaking Shakespeare and it was a wonderful lesson in learning how to handle this language.

In *The Two Gentlemen of Verona*, Ian played Proteus and I played his servant Launce, who has the dog, Crab. Ian was very funny in this character and it was the first chance I had to see him playing comedy. And I relished watching him playing a romantic lead for once and he was outstanding.

There was always that slight touch of grand Scottishness about him as well – some of which I used recently when I played Malvolio as a rather arrogant Edinburgh type. There was always that hint of superiority about Ian's accent that I always imagined was the Scot in him.

I had a foundling dog called Blackie that I hadn't wanted because I preferred to have something outlandish, but at the pound they kept telling me to take this dog. It was just a black dog growing grey at the muzzle and it looked incredibly uninteresting. But what a personality this dog had and I learnt so much about concentration, listening and focus from it.

The dog didn't like Ian's character – or perhaps it was Ian – and when he was on, the dog regarded him rather suspiciously. There was one moment in the play where Ian was abusing both me and my dog. The dog would turn its back on Ian, put its chin on the floor and stick its bum up Ian's nose, which stopped the show – this happened several times. And of course Ian loved this and would react marvellously to it.

In my second year I found myself with a lot of time on my hands and John Barton asked me if I'd like to be put into his recital programme, *The Hollow Crown*. I wanted to do it because I'd seen it and thought it was wonderful. What this gave me the opportunity to do was to go regularly to John Barton's flat and get master classes. Ian was one of the people regularly doing *The Hollow Crown*. We did a lot of touring round the country and we had this van we would all go off in and it would be myself, Ian, Sue Fleetwood, sometimes Janet Suzman, Tony Church and Martin

Best playing the guitar and lute and we would perform this brilliant programme. Ian doing his Walpole and the James I counterblast against tobacco was absolutely glorious in terms of timing and precision.

Ian became quite friendly and looked out for me and there was a time when he and Maroussia loaned me their flat near the British Museum in Bloomsbury. He was always warm and supportive and such a fine mentor for a young actor.

The last time I saw him was at a 40th Anniversary Gala for the Yvonne Arnaud Theatre in Guildford in November 2005. Ian closed the first half with Prospero's 'Our revels now are ended' speech and it was wonderful – a very suitable memory.

—◆◆◆—

Estelle Kohler – Actress

Working with Ian was always fun and entertaining. He was the most adorable, inventive, kindly, loving acting partner I had in all those years at the RSC. We worked closely together on many productions, including *Measure for Measure, Love's Labour's Lost, All's Well that Ends Well, Coriolanus* and *The Tempest* – every single one was a pleasure.

As well as his invention, I enjoyed very much Ian's amazing speed with the verse. Even if he dropped a line, he never dropped a beat – and to mix several metaphors, always managed somehow to get out of trouble by weaving and knitting his way back onto the piste.

In *Measure for Measure*, Ian played Angelo and I played Isabella. In rehearsals, it developed that he dragged me across the floor by the hair – terrifying to watch. In actual fact, technically, the dragger grabs a handful of hair while the victim apparently in panic, grabs the hand of the dragger in a struggle to relieve the pain. No strain is actually applied to the hair itself; the victim is simply pulled by the hand.

Ian was an extremely technical actor, interpretively, vocally and physically, so anything like dragging someone by the hair was always rehearsed carefully and safely, however violent it may have appeared in performance. I believe I was dragged by my hair more often than most actresses – and Ian dragged me consummately.

Terence Rigby – Actor

(Terence, sadly, passed away not long after providing his contribution)

In 1964 I had travelled to Stratford-Upon-Avon to spend a day or two with Michael Jayston. On the train I met R D (Reggie) Smith, the immensely famous, renowned BBC Radio Producer. On trains with Reggie, you never took to a seat – you stood in the bar for the entire journey, not able to get much of a word in, listening, fascinated, to him – and getting thoroughly plastered along the way.

Later, well on the way to oblivion, I found myself in the Dirty Duck in Stratford, surrounded by many of the Company as well as Peter Brook, when Ian stepped in, immaculately dressed as always. He didn't know me from Adam, as I had just joined the London end at the Aldwych. As he came in, I was turning and managed to collide with him and tip a full pint jug of beer all down his front and was naturally horrified, as I recognised him immediately.

Expecting the Wrath of God to pour from him, I was

staggered almost beyond words as he dusted himself down with a beautifully clean handkerchief, declining my abject apologies and inferring that it was he who had been responsible for the collision.

The next year, the RSC were touring, in repertoire, *The Two Gentlemen of Verona* – to be joined by the world premiere of Pinter's *The Homecoming*, in which I appeared as Joey.

We were in Cardiff. Both Ian and Michael Williams had leading roles in *Verona* and shared a dressing room. During 'the half' I popped in to see Michael, whom I knew from my days at RADA. Ian was getting himself a drink – life backstage was rather different during those years. It seems that the local dresser had not arrived or was late.

When Ian returned and saw me in the room, he lashed into me for being inexcusably late and as he had several tricky changes, immediately began to list them very, very quickly. Meanwhile, Michael was roaring away with laughter and trying at the same time to inform Ian that he had made an embarrassing error and that I was a member of the Pinter cast. When the dust settled, Ian was horrified and just could not stop apologising. I decided though, to exit before the real dresser arrived.

Ian was never, in my experience, an actor of the gregarious social set which prevailed during the 60's and 70's. The fact is he was always too busy working – constantly developing his great talent.

—◦◦◦—

Roger Lloyd Pack – Actor

One of my first jobs as an actor was playing small

parts at the RSC in 1967, at a time when Ian had just established prominence with the Company. The previous year he had scored a big personal success in *The Revenger's Tragedy* and this was repeated the season I was there. He also played the lead in *Coriolanus* and Malcolm in Paul Scofield's *Macbeth*. I was in all three of these productions, but as a very junior member.

Sheila, my wife to be at that time, was his dresser for the season and because of that relationship we were quite friendly with Ian and Maroussia and I remember hanging out with Maroussia and their two children, who were then quite small.

I have a very clear image of him playing Coriolanus, standing very erect and commanding, one leg straight, the other leg straight but at an angle. He spoke the text very clearly and had great stillness. There was a precision about his acting that was very particular.

—···—

David Weston – Actor

I first met Ian Richardson in 1967 when I understudied his Coriolanus at Stratford. I was also playing Titus Lartius so I had the opportunity of studying him deeply. Some critic said at the time he was the most Senecan of British actors. I can still see him standing fearlessly centre stage, one arm thrust into his waist, faultlessly delivering speech after speech, night after night.

Off stage he always seemed exhausted – he was also playing Bertram in *All's Well* and Malcolm in Scofield's disastrous *Macbeth* as well as Vendice in *The Revenger's Tragedy* – but he never missed a performance, despite being wounded several times by the erratic swordsmanship of Aufidius [played by American actor, Edward Ciccarelli].

Mike Leigh was the Assistant Director and he and I had done a lot of work together on my understudy but I never came near to getting on. I was touched to read in an obituary that Coriolanus was one of the roles of which Ian was most proud.

At that time Peter Hall's new RSC had spawned three major talents – David Warner, Ian Holm and Ian Richardson. In 1967 David had already played Hamlet and Richard II and was off making movies – the ultimate aim of most actors then and now. Ian Holm had had a great success in Pinter on Broadway and was restless and couldn't wait to go, but Ian R seemed keener on establishing himself as the RSC's leading actor.

Unlike many leading RSC actors he seemed to accept any role that was offered. Malcolm was not cast at the beginning of the season. I had hopes of playing it myself as I had already played him in the Scofield/Peggy Ashcroft radio version, as well as having had good notices in a production at the Mermaid a few years previously. Malcolm is not a very rewarding part for a leading actor but Ian actively sought out the role.

Macbeth was scheduled to tour the world but it was fated from the start. Peter Hall contracted shingles, rehearsals were suspended and although he came back it was to be his final production in his stewardship of the RSC.

We took the production to Finland and Russia in the depths of winter. I recall going with Ian and a handful of others to visit Stanislavsky's house in Moscow. We were shown around by his old valet, who had survived fifty years of Communism. Ian was enchanted by him and he was enchanted by Ian – perhaps seeing in Ian's elegant manner echoes of the aristocratic past.

Ian stayed with the RSC for several years after I left, playing Richard II at last. I next met him one cold morning at the Chadwick Street Labour Exchange, as it was called in those days. Ian, accompanied by Maroussia, stood in line to sign on, bearing himself like a prince, although I noticed his shoes were very down at the heel. I'd heard that they were pretty hard up for a time – having to live off discarded vegetables from the market. [Ian was out of work for a year after leaving the RSC and he and Maroussia used to join the nuns, collecting bruised vegetables at Covent Garden to make soup].

I saw him give one of his most brilliant performances in *The Government Inspector* at the Old Vic and shortly after he had established himself as a television star.

The last time I saw him was several months before his death, in *The Alchemist* at the National. Ian shone like a silver fox.

3

He Who Plays the King

One of the most celebrated RSC productions of the Seventies was *Richard II*, in which the roles of Richard and Bolingbroke were alternated by Ian and Richard Pasco. It was the first time the two actors had worked together and proved to be an extremely happy and successful collaboration:

> "Dickie played Richard more elegiacally – he was the martyr king, he was the Christ figure. I told John Barton that I didn't see Richard II as the figure of Jesus Christ on the Cross, which Dickie did. John said, 'That's wonderful – we want these changes. What do you see him as?' I responded, 'Well, I have to tell you that I think of Richard II as an actor. He just performs – beautifully. He has all the best speeches in the play and he does them to the hilt. What is more, if you look at the play, he is never ever alone. He always has an audience until he is in prison. That's the only time he is on his own.'
>
> So I played him as a showman – the bigger the audience, the bigger the king, which meant that he had the further to fall, and a lot of people didn't go along with that because Dickie and I shared the roles of Richard and Bolingbroke, from performance to performance. There were people who paid to see Dickie who would not pay

to see me playing the king and vice versa.

I remember on one occasion, we both came out of our dressing rooms wearing the Richard II wigs, which were slightly more glamorous than the Bolingbroke ones. I said, 'Oh God, Dickie.' We went down to the stage director and said 'Who is the king this afternoon?' He didn't know and said that he'd better ring the Box Office. They'd sold most tickets for the matinee, so I said to Dickie, 'Right, you'd better play the king.'

It was a very odd experience altogether, because we both knew all the dialogue for the king and also for Bolingbroke. There was one performance at which Dickie had been the king in the afternoon and I was the king at night. I was sitting on the throne with my orb and sceptre, and the crown on my head. Dickie was down there at my feet, playing Bolingbroke and he dried up. He could not remember the line. Now, I had played that part in the afternoon, but I couldn't think what the line he needed was. I could not help him nor prompt him. I've never forgotten that – it was quite staggering in a way, that we were completely divorced from what we had done just a few hours before. And we never mixed up our lines.

The only time I mixed up Shakespearian roles – and it wasn't surprising – I was playing Cassius the conspirator in *Julius Caesar* in the evening and I was filming *A Midsummer Night's Dream* out at Compton Verney during the day. At night, I had to say towards the end of the performance in *Julius Caesar*, 'Go, Pindarus, get thou higher on that hill and tell me what thou noticed upon the field' (meaning the field of battle). I said to this boy, 'Go, Pindarus, get thee higher on that hill and be thou here again ere the Leviathan could swim a league,' which went straight from Cassius into Oberon. Now he, Pindarus, didn't notice a thing, nor did the audience, but I noticed. My character was about to commit suicide and I was helpless with laughter."

Nickolas Grace – Actor

As a child I'd regularly been taken to Stratford to see the plays and the RSC was always my ideal dream Company. I moved to London and went to the Aldwych from 1963 onwards and saw Ian in everything – he was extraordinary.

I joined the RSC in 1972. Richard Pasco took me under his wing initially and became my mentor. I remember being called into Trevor Nunn's office with John Barton and was told that they'd like me to play Aumerle in *Richard II.* When he described his concept for the play to us on the first day, we went out laughing. He'd told us that there would be two escalators on stage and that there would be two Richards and two Bolingbrokes.

We had eight weeks to rehearse and watching them both play off each other was just extraordinary. As Richard, Dickie Pasco was the more straight-forward less flamboyant king and Ian was far more the histrionic Richard. What always struck me was Ian's tremendous vocal pyrotechnics.

Playing Aumerle to his Richard we became quite close and he said to me, "I think we should go out to lunch and have a chat." He took me out to a restaurant and we bonded and became quite close. He used to send me lots of notes, starting, 'Nick, Dear'. He loved sending notes because then he wouldn't have to go through John Barton.

Ian became this extraordinary decadent, flamboyant Richard and in a way it was the other way round with Bolingbroke. It was a real honour to watch both Ian and Dickie on stage. It was a brilliant concept by John Barton.

He was a great joker. I remember, just before the deposition scene, he would be standing upstage and he'd pull a face and I thought, 'He can't be,' but he was because he knew he could then get the next 'c' sharp note technically. There were times in *Richard II* when his antics would have me trying desperately not to laugh, without success.

Ian was always walking that fine line and he could do ambiguity very well. I remember in *Richard II*, there was the sequence from the battlements. By that stage we were pretty close and Ian and Dickie would do things in different ways. One day, on tour, Ian told me he was going to go a little further – exploring the sexual frisson between our characters. It came to the first performance in the Brooklyn Academy of Arts. Ian said, "Aumerle, my tender-hearted cousin, thou weepest." And I used to cry because I was so carried away with it. He lifted a tear from my cheek, looked at it and kissed it and I thought, 'My God, they're not going to miss that'.

I learnt so much as an actor from the way he spoke Shakespeare. And he was so helpful and constructive. I believe he was a prime example of what the RSC was, at its best. He was a real ensemble member who grew through the Company, became one of the leading members and a star of the Royal Shakespeare Company and of television and film.

Juliet Stevenson – Actress

Seeing Ian on stage for the first time in *Richard II* was part of a lot of firsts all rolled into one. It was the first time I'd been to Stratford, the first thing I'd seen by the Royal Shakespeare Company and the first full-length proper production of a Shakespeare play in a theatre I'd seen.

I was 16 or 17 at the time and I went with some school friends. It was somebody's birthday and her parents were taking a group of girls to Stratford as a treat.

It was one of the very, very few occurrences that you have in your childhood or adolescence that are a kind of quantum leap and you never get them again. It was one of those intense experiences you have when you are growing up which changes everything in a moment. I walked into the theatre that evening one person and came out as another person. That was very largely due to Ian.

He was playing Richard that night and I saw the production six times – five times with Ian as Richard and Richard Pasco as Bolingbroke and once the other way around. I thought I'd better see him as Bolingbroke but I couldn't stand it that way.

Ian was a really brilliant actor in a kind of mould that I'm not sure is going to go on existing. He bridged two generations in acting – the generation before him, was the Gielgud/Richardson/Olivier generation, which I was never in love with. For me personally, they were too sung, too mannered and I never believed in them, even as a child because I could see the cogs, however skilful they were. I've never wanted to be impressed – to be shown how wonderful someone's performance is and that was my instinct from very early on.

But Ian bridged that somehow because he was quite mannered and he was heightened but everything came from the centre. He could be enormous because it always came from some absolute reality in the centre of him and it was like an extension of a psychological truth or complicated cocktail of truths and I think that Richard was an extraordinary creation.

I've never seen another performance of the role come near it and I think he was consummate because he embodied some fantastic combination of contradictions in that character between superficiality and vanity and the profundity of the journey that he goes on. Self-pity and a sort of nobility, self-absorption and finally a kind of wisdom. He was prosaic and poetic – male and female. I fell completely and utterly in love with him because he was very, very sexy. It wasn't obvious because it was quite hermaphrodite and I think that was part of the attraction. His Richard was quite camp but it was also very sexy.

He had a phenomenal relationship with the spoken verse and made it seem effortless, though I'm sure it wasn't. There was a small handful of actors who could make it seem so – Alan Howard was one and Ian was another. The musicality and rhythms of the blank verse were so mastered that he could play with it because it was so in his bones.

It was completely revelatory. What interest would a sixteen year-old girl from the south of England have in a beleaguered king who was usurped and holed up in a castle – who cared? But Ian made me care so much and affected me so profoundly that I couldn't think of anyone else but Richard II all that summer. I remember going on a family holiday to Scotland for a few weeks and I just locked myself in my room and learnt the whole part of Richard II and even now, thirty years on, I could still recite whole chunks of it.

It opened many doors for me. I got what verse speaking was and I got what Shakespeare was. A whole lot of doors blew open. I don't think I'm the kind of actor he was, but I can feel his influence on me.

My plan was to go to university but as it got nearer, I

thought I'd read drama. I got a place in Bristol to do drama and then I wondered, 'What am I going to do at the other end – I don't want to be a drama teacher?' I wrote to Ian, pretending to be a drama student rather than a schoolgirl, and asked if I should join the profession or not. He wrote this rather lofty but sweet reply and said something like, "Well, dear thing, if you must, you must – but it's an infuriating profession." I thought that was rather grand, but not terribly helpful. In the end I decided not to go to Bristol and went to RADA.

I was always hoping I'd get the chance to meet and work with him one day and tell him. And then I finally got that chance when we did a recital programme of Shakespearian sonnets at a literary festival in Cheltenham in 2004. We were driven back to London together and I did get the opportunity to tell him. He must have thought that I was terribly gushy, but I'm very glad I did and I should imagine he might have been quite chuffed.

It was absolutely thrilling to be working with him – he never waned. Some actors deteriorate – they stop taking risks, or learning or continue to produce the same versions of themselves. Ian never got into that – he was always as brilliant, as sharp and as creative as ever. I just remember being on stage that afternoon and being humbled and thinking, 'Oh dear, I've got to get up and follow that.'

He was so funny – there was hardly anybody in this country who could be funnier than him on stage or on screen.

Ian spent his last few years with the RSC playing, amongst others, Iachimo in *Cymbeline*, Scholz in Wedekind's *The Marquis of Keith* and Ford again in *The Merry Wives of Windsor*. His final part was the lead in *Richard III*.

In 1973, Ian played Berowne, in *Love's Labour's Lost,* in which The King of Navarre allows Berowne and two fellow noblemen to study at court, providing they pledge themselves to three years of studying, fasting, very little sleep and total avoidance of women.

It was an extremely challenging, but ultimately joyful role for Ian:

"Berowne, the role that became my all-time favourite, came to me when I was almost into my forties. I was very excited about it but found it very difficult to memorise because Shakespeare had written it for himself. He wrote a real *tour de force* of verbal witticisms and he can never use one adjective if he can produce six. I realised that the only way to play it was very rapidly.

I was trying so desperately to cram all this beautiful convoluted verse into my head that I suddenly panicked when the first preview was upon us. At the end of the rehearsal that morning, in a state of abject terror and despair, I went to Holy Trinity Church and up to Shakespeare's tomb. I looked up and asked him for his help.

When I said my first line of the evening I got my first big laugh and said a silent, 'Thank you, Will.' I just loved Berowne – partly because he was a lovely chap and partly because I knew that he was the last juvenile part I was ever likely to play."

Reviewing the play in *Plays and Players,* October 1973, Garry O'Connor commented, "Ian Richardson must be one of the very few actors of recent years to make his name with those conventional drama school qualities of a fine, beautifully modulated voice, marvellous stance, and a rare and excellent sense of timing. His Berowne is the essence of boyish exuberance. His resources of optimistic goodwill appear endless. Some are born with silver spoons in their mouths, Mr Richardson was born with the iambic pentameter. He warbles, he flutes, he moans, he juggles, he transposes, stands on his head, lies on his back: whatever he may be doing, the lines ring out with clarity and precision."

——◆◆◆——

Nickolas Grace

Ian was very reluctant to do *Love's Labour's Lost*, playing Berowne – he just didn't think he was getting it. He used to moan to me that he was hating it and just couldn't learn it. But I went to a preview and it was one of the greatest things I've ever seen because that was the real vocal pyrotechnics. He did the whole thing at about a hundred miles an hour. It was like an express train – he did it really rapidly but you could hear every single word and he got a clap after the first speech. He was staggering.

He was a tremendous ad libber and it all made sense because he kept it going by just talking in iambic pentameter. Ian was probably the greatest exponent of speaking Shakespeare colloquially – he could chuck it away and make it colloquial and at other times he could make the verse sound like gold dust.

——◆◆◆——

Sir Ian McKellen – Actor
10 February 2007 – Reproduced, with kind permission, from Ian McKellen's website

Over a decade or more, Richardson was a shining star at Stratford for the RSC. When I played the Brooklyn Academy of Music in 1974, where he had just shared Richard II and Bolingbroke with Richard Pasco on an RSC tour, I was mistaken for him a couple of times.

The next year we were both cast in *The Marquis of*

Keith, again for the RSC. It is not an easy play and mine was a fiendish part. Richardson as ever was effortlessly in charge of his own, whilst I floundered, even to the extent of forgetting my lines at a number of performances. At each shameful dry, Ian helped me through by providing a subtle prompt and although he must have disapproved of what can only be called 'an error in stagecraft', he never showed it. He was a company man and a gentleman.

He was most famous for his voice, which could mellifluously flute or bellow – an instrument that any Lear would envy. Of late he regretted that he wasn't much considered for the great roles he was fitted to play and said something to the effect that 'Lear only goes to people like McKellen these days'.

He hid what perhaps he felt to be a failing: his height. A few inches short of six feet, he always wore lifts hidden within his shoes on stage. Yet he needn't have worried. Striding on as Vendice, Richard III, Angelo or Richard II, he seemed as imposing as the tallest of actors. Within him was the fire and the power. It exploded in the jealousy of his magnificent Ford in *The Merry Wives of Windsor* just as effectively as in the tragic roles. If only he had played King Lear.

David Suchet – Actor

When I joined the Royal Shakespeare Company in 1973 I had the great privilege to be in the production of *Richard II*. I was a very junior member of the Company and was boot boy to Sebastian Shaw's Duke of York, and a spear carrier. It was in the latter role that I found myself standing with a group of other spear carriers behind Ian as he delivered the memorable speech beginning with the words:

Boat to Tighnabruiach

Courting Days, outside the Dirty Duck in Stratford

Wedding Day, 2 February, 1961.
© Michael Ward

I

With Elizabeth Spriggs, in *The Merry Wives of Windsor*
The Thos F. and Mig Holte Collection © Shakespeare Birthplace Trust

As Marat in the filmed
version of *Marat/Sade*

Alas poor Yorick! Performing the speech for
the *Civilisation* series in 1969

Ian R as Oberon and Ian Holm as Puck
in the *A Midsummer Night's Dream* film

Ian as Angelo, with Estelle Kohler as
Isabella in *Measure for Measure*
© Reg C Wilson, Royal Shakespeare Company

Two Gentlemen of Verona Rehearsal with Helen Mirren
© Zoe Dominic

Berowne in *Love's Labour's Lost*
Joe Cocks Studio Collection © Shakespeare Birthplace Trust

With Richard Pasco in *Richard II*
Joe Cocks Studio Collection ©, Shakespeare Birthplace Trust

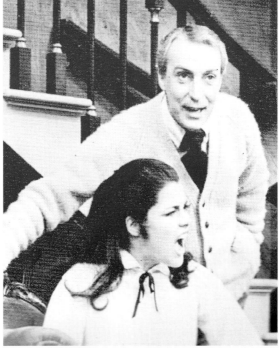

Bill Haydon in *Tinker Tailor Soldier Spy*

The Great Detective, Sherlock Holmes

The Master of Ballantrae

Sam Dastor, Ian, producer Judith de Paul and Indian Prime Minister Indira Gandhi

As Sir Godber Evans in Porterhouse Blue, with David Jason as Scullion, 1987

An Ungentlemanly Act,
with Rosemary Leach

Troubles with Ian Charleson

'For God's sake let us sit upon the ground
And tell sad stories of the death of Kings'

It is a most wonderful speech and Ian spoke it beautifully. So beautifully, in fact, that one evening I became so rapt in his delivery that I let slip my spear from my hand and it landed right beside him with a great thud. I remember to this day his disdainful look at the spear by his side. As unobtrusively as I possibly could, I picked it up.

Later on that evening I was summoned to dressing room number one and asked to explain myself. Ian was the perfect gentleman. He was kind and understanding and I am sure he could sense my knees were trembling beneath my costume.

I worked with Ian on several occasions after and it was a great privilege.

—◆◆—

Charles Dance – Actor

I met Ian when I joined the Royal Shakespeare Company in 1975. I had the good fortune to play Catesby in Barry Kyle's production of *Richard III* at The Other Place. I had been aware of him and his wonderful work for years and to finally act with him was the most instructive joy imaginable. Of the many consummate actors we have in Britain, Ian was the most consummate. He was blessed with a wonderful voice and a range that could have an audience falling about at his comic gifts and chilled to the bone when he was being villainous.

Despite being at the pinnacle of his profession he was never 'grand' or aloof. His advice, whenever he was asked to proffer it, was never dispensed 'from a great height' but just passed on to whoever was fortunate enough to receive it, in a spirit of humility and genuine desire to help. And he was never patronising.

Despite his wonderful theatrical flair, he was as masterful in front of a camera as he was on a stage. He knew the virtue of stillness and economy in front of a searching lens – witness his chilling portrayal of Robespierre in *Danton's Death* – not a muscle in his face moved, just those eyes and a coldly modulated liquid voice telling us everything.

—◆◆◆—

Jacqueline Chnéour – Former Technical Interpreter and Dresser, RSC

I was there. I was there, night after night, matinee after matinee, in the dark and womb-like auditorium of the Royal Shakespeare Theatre, standing at the back of the stalls, leaning on my railing, lapping it all up: the scenery, the costumes, the music, the verse, the emotions. I was there when Ian Richardson was a god and he knew it and he had the audience hanging on his every inflection, when his voice soared... ah!... *Every* review of *every* play he was in mentioned the voice, but this is what Roger Lewis said in his book *Stage People* (Weidenfeld & Nicholson, 1989):

"He sings his sentences, his voice swooping from a bellow to a whisper, from a hoot to a silence. Richardson's voice is his instrument; he is conscious of it and proud of it; he plays upon it and with it. He can draw out a single word into an alarming stutter of syllables, like a libretto fragmented and reproduced under the stave; he'll then speed ahead, putting a girdle around a paragraph in four seconds."

It *was* the voice above all. But also the poise, the

42

stillness. And the wit. And the sense of danger too. There, on the stage, not preserved in aspic for posterity.

I lived in the Richardsons' Stratford house, with two other girls, for the best part of 1974. He wasn't there; he was renting it out to us. There was a throne from some past RSC production on the patio; Marat's tin bath was rusting at the bottom of the garden; his acting editions of Penguin Shakespeare were sitting on the shelves in the living room. Fans used to walk past the house, stop and point at it.

When I was working as a dresser at the Aldwych Theatre we used to pass each other backstage every night and exchange no more than a smile, except once, when he said something so bitchy about someone we both knew that I was in hysterics for the rest of the evening.

When I think of Ian Richardson, I think of Pericles, looking frail on that big stage; I think of Richard II, looking like a beautiful golden bird ready to take flight; I think of Berowne and his breakneck and hilarious delivery; I think of Angelo pulling Isabella's hair in that terrible scene; I think of... oh, too many memories...

There was a sense that anything could happen when he was on stage (which must have been quite disconcerting for the other actors, although he never deliberately upstaged). When he was playing Bolingbroke, for a while he used to hurl himself on to Richard's coffin from the throne, whilst uttering a very, very long cry of woe. The throne was high up on the stage, on a platform with steps. I was there when he did it for the first time – the audience gasped but so did the technicians. He didn't do it for very long, but it was spectacular.

He could mesmerize the audience and he was a

brilliant ad libber. I once witnessed him, in *Cymbeline*, graciously bowing and thanking a woman in the front row of the RST without missing a beat in his long speech. She had picked up Iachimo's ring (essential to the plot), which he had accidentally dropped and had placed it carefully – and rapidly – on the edge of the stage. It was a veritable *tour de force* that won him a round of applause.

There were so many similar moments that took one's breath away.

4

Life Beyond Shakespeare

Eyeless in Gaza – 1971

"I had enormous admiration for him, which I had to try and curb in order to direct him." That was the experience of director James Cellan Jones when he first worked with Ian, who was on a two-year break from the RSC, and playing Anthony Beavis, the main role in the BBC adaptation of Aldous Huxley's *Eyeless in Gaza*.

James Cellan Jones – Director

When Ian did *Eyeless in Gaza* it was just about his first television role. I thought that we were very lucky to get him and I think he found it very intriguing to do something so totally different from what he'd done till then. It was a terribly complex role. Anthony Beavis described himself as a sociologist and sociology wasn't used much then, so Huxley had to churn out a lot of pseudo-psychological stuff which Ian had to spout.

We went to Portugal, which doubled for the South of France and Mexico. I was doing a long tracking shot of Ian and John Laurie riding mules along a narrow defile. Because they were riding abreast, the shot was rather wide. Cunning old John said, "I'll get off and lead this puir auld beast – she's finding it a wee bit hard going," thus turning the shot into deep two shot, with himself large in the foreground and Ian out of focus in the distance. Ian, who rode beautifully and behaved perfectly, didn't complain at all, knowing that I would take close ups of him later, which I did.

We shot a lot of riding sequences in Portugal; and then it began to rain incessantly. We were still missing a lot of close-ups of the two actors on mules; we eventually shot them in my back garden with the actors sitting on stools and pretending to hold the reins and bouncing up and down.

Not long before, I had worked with Michael Gambon at the Birmingham Rep and I cast him in *Eyeless.* He was not well known at the time and a rather junior member of the cast. When he did the speech from Rochester, 'Now old age and experience hand in hand...' Ian said, "This boy is going to be very, very good." He had an extremely generous nature.

We did a scene where Beavis was forced by a barman to drink tequila (which of course was really water) and it was meant to make him shake. Ian couldn't quite get it right, so I swapped the water for some real tequila. He swallowed it and his eyes nearly popped out – it was a wonderfully funny reaction.

We got on extremely well right from the start. Ian would occasionally have Shakespearian lapses and I would say to him, "Stop saying that, you very foolish person," and he would laugh. We used to send each other up dreadfully.

—◆◆◆—

Man of La Mancha

Another break from the RSC came with the filming of the United Artists musical, *Man of La Mancha*, in which Ian played the priest, in 1972. Amongst the cast were Peter O'Toole as Don Quixote, Sophia Loren as Dulcinea, James Coco as Sancho Panza and Brian Blessed as Pedro, the Head Muleteer.

Brian Blessed – Pedro

When we were filming *Man of La Mancha*, I was taking the actors and the composer Laurence Rosenthal up the mountains whilst we were in Italy. All the actors wanted to come with me and climb the mountains and have adventures but Ian declined. "You'll never get me up there, Brian. For God's sake, I'll have a heart attack!"

I only had to look at Ian and he went into hysterics. I was always very naughty with him and it would have him in fits of laughter. Basically, he was a Peter Pan character and he had a wonderful sense of humour.

Ian played the priest wonderfully and with great sensitivity – and he had a lovely singing voice, which I think should have been used much more in musicals. His priest is so moving and it was a gem of a performance.

He loved imitating Arthur Lucan as Old Mother Riley [Lucan created the Irish washerwoman character initially for the Music Hall and went on to play her in 16 films between 1937 and 1952]. They were very comical films and Ian would imitate her brilliantly. He would drop his jaw and his face would contort into Mother Riley and this sophisticated actor would turn into a ridiculous comedian. In between scenes he would become Mother Riley (and sometimes forget to come out of character when filming).

I remember once, we were in the studios and they'd failed to collect his wife from Rome airport and he went absolutely ballistic – effing and blinding and threatening to walk out. Maroussia was so precious to him and the relationship was wonderfully special. He was extremely sensitive, but come hell or high water he would defend her against the world.

He was always impressed by me being a mountaineer and an explorer and he is one of the few actors I really got on with and we were deeply fond of one another. We shared a great love of the classics and knowledge of Shakespeare and we adored each other's sense of humour.

My Fair Lady

Having finally left the RSC in 1975, Ian went to New York to star as Henry Higgins in the 20th Anniversary Broadway revival of *My Fair Lady*. The show, with Christine Andreas as Eliza Doolittle, Robert Coote as Colonel Pickering and George Rose as Alfred P Doolittle, ran for a year. His performance was highly acclaimed and gained him a Drama Desk Award and a Tony Nomination.

Christine Andreas – Actress – Eliza Doolittle

I was introduced to Ian by our producer, Herman Levin, in the lobby of the Algonquin Hotel in 1975, a few months before rehearsals started for *My Fair Lady*. From the first moment of meeting, he was generous and the most gentlemanly man I had ever met. I knew of his fame and I was horribly aware of my inexperience.

We had no time at all to get this beautiful show together for Broadway. I was blissfully unaware of this in my ignorance, but 3 weeks rehearsal and 3 weeks previewing for a show of this scale was daunting to the seasoned pros. Looking back, the kindness, generosity and PATIENCE of Ian and the entire company awaiting the birth of my 'Eliza' was profound!

At one point, out of town in Philadelphia, Pennsylvania, I recall the agony I was experiencing with the 'slipper scene'. It was torture – I just didn't 'get it.' I cut myself a little slack and told myself, "This is Shaw, folks and I am an unschooled actor but with a flexible, lovely natural voice that is getting me a lot of attention." I remember one night, the scene was suddenly effortless – it all just fell together in that mysterious way things can when we stop forcing and pushing and worst of all 'watching' ourselves in action.

Ian was the first to exit stage and when I exited stage right I remember looking down and there was a red carpet under my feet that was laid all the way to my dressing room. How did Ian do that?

I will never know, but I had a year of gallantry with Ian Richardson that I will never forget.

Alex Jennings – Actor – Henry Higgins in the National Theatre Revival of My Fair Lady

I had the disc of Ian as Higgins in *My Fair Lady* and that was in my ears when I did it. I thought he was just dazzling. The speed that he played it at meant that his was the performance I revered. And he played me the greatest compliment by saying that he'd love to play Pickering to my Henry Higgins if I ever played *My Fair Lady* again.

Tinker Tailor Soldier Spy

In 1979, Ian got the chance to play Bill Haydon in the award-winning adaptation of John Le Carré's tense Cold War spy thriller, *Tinker Tailor Soldier Spy*. It was a stunning performance, particularly in the scenes in which he and Sir Alec Guinness, playing George Smiley, acted together.

Having worked almost exclusively in the theatre for 20 years, he realised that it was most definitely time for a change:

"Until *Tinker Tailor* came along I'd been exclusively a theatre actor. I'd come back from Canada, where I'd been playing in Bernard Shaw's *Man and Superman* at the Festival Theatre in Ontario, previously doing the revival of *My Fair Lady* in New York. I said to my agent that I'd had enough of long runs recreating the same performance eight times a week for months. I asked her to get me into television. She said it wouldn't be easy because I didn't have any television reputation.

About this time, I attended a memorial service for a lovely old British actor called Leo Genn and reading the address, was Sir Alec Guinness. Afterwards I walked up and congratulated him on how nicely he'd done it and he looked at me and said, 'Do I know you?' I said, 'I think you do but perhaps not for a while, because I've been out of the country,' and he said, 'Ah yes, Richardson.' Two days later the scripts of *Tinker Tailor* arrived on my doorstep. I think Alec, in his quite justifiable position as the leading actor of the series, had casting control and he probably told the director he thought he should get Richardson to play the mole.

Because I played such an eye-catching part as it was in the end, though not to begin with – the director deliberately kept my screen appearances to a minimum so that the audience wouldn't guess who the villain was

- when it came to the last scenes, there we were. And that was the launch of my career as a television actor."

—◆◆◆—

John Irvin – Director

My sense of Ian before working with him was of a very fine classical actor who had done great work at the RSC and who had enormous power and terrific gifts. That made him a contender for the role of Bill Haydon.

When you are casting it's like you are choosing colours for a palette. What I did, was cast five distinctive actors with different personae who would bounce off each other. It's not simply a case of casting a great actor – you've got to select actors who complement each other, represent enough contrast and are standouts. The thing about Ian was that he had a standout talent, but he also, within the context of the Circus in *Tinker Tailor*, was obviously going to be a great contrast to the other members of the higher echelons of the organisation.

I cast them because you have to convince the audience that these people had brains and are clever, intellectual people – they are not James Bonds. They are cerebral men with first class minds and it's difficult to cast actors who are convincing as intellectuals. They have to have interior lives and the actors have to get that across.

Ian was striking in that department and the fact that he was better known on stage – particularly on the classical stage – didn't matter too much, certainly to me, because he was a consummate actor and my job was to internalise his performance. On the other hand – and that's why it was such a clever performance – his character had to be rather flamboyant and a bit of

51

a showman without going over the top and the part required him to be something of a character.

His first rehearsal was really quite funny because he was so expressive, and poor Alec retreated into his shell. He felt like he was being bombarded by mortar fire. I remember when Ian shouted at Alec and Alec just looked back at him. He was shell-shocked by all this noise and flamboyance. They both had the same agent and Alec rang her up after the rehearsal and asked if Ian was always like that. He received the reply, "He won't be tomorrow."

I took him aside and told him what the camera could do and that he should just relax. We sorted it out and they were very complementary.

The scenes near the end with Alec and Ian were so strong – absolutely terrific. They showed the banality of Haydon's character. He was an intellectual and social snob and a bully, but at the same time he was a little vulnerable and patently misguided and his personality had been somewhat distorted by his ambition and his rage. It was such a complex role and Ian inhabited it very well. He cottoned on to the technical requirements for the small screen very quickly – it's about the mental process as well as the physical and is a concentration of effort rather than an expansion of it.

Ian was a great collaborator and once he became comfortable with the environment, which was a little unfamiliar to him, he loved it. He did jump in but was very patient and relished the role and just enjoyed the fun of playing Bill Haydon. He realised the power of the cameras and he went off to do more great stuff and embrace the medium and it suited him really well. It was a very happy cast and company. Ian was wonderful and I retained a huge affection and admiration for him. And of course I saw him often with Maroussia and their relationship was a very close, tender, caring and respectful one.

Terence Rigby – Roy Bland

It was the largest read through on Day One that you could imagine. Every character from the five episodes was present, making it an extraordinary occasion. To name but a few, Sir Alec Guinness, Ian, Sian Phillips, Bernard Hepton, Michael Jayston and Ian Bannen. It was shot 'as film' which meant that we only met thereafter in groups depending on the day's shooting.

One lasting memory, was that every time I arrived at the side of the set, Ian (and invariably Maroussia) would be seated with Sir Alec – who but rarely spoke – in deep, long conversation. Clearly Ian was anxious to soak up the knowledge of the great actor as much as he possibly could and certainly he would have done just that.

Old Vic Theatre Company

Ian gave his last stage performances in the UK for 16 years when he played Khlestakov in *The Government Inspector* and Mercutio in *Romeo and Juliet* at the Old Vic, in 1979.

Peter Stothard, writing in the August 1979 edition of *Plays and Players*, was scathing in his assessment of the overall production of *Romeo and Juliet* but did comment, "Mercutio, however, is one of the few lead parts in Shakespeare which an actor can take, knowing that however dreadful the production, he can always give a respectable performance. Ian Richardson plays

Romeo's friend and tormentor in the most consummately created void, with dead eyes and a piercing dead wit, disdainful of everything around."

Ian recognised the fact that the villainous role of Mercutio was far more interesting than that of the supposed hero, Romeo, a view shared by others.

A member of the public, providing a memory on the BBC News Online website tribute to Ian after his death commented, "I remember seeing him as Mercutio in *Romeo and Juliet* at the New Theatre in Hull – a school trip, as we were studying the play. Although he was in his mid-forties at the time, his wit and sparkle won the hearts of our class of teenage girls more than the youthful charms (and tights) of Romeo, Paris and co. There was weeping in the stalls when Tybalt killed him."

Barbara Jefford – Actress

I was in both in *Romeo and Juliet* and *The Government Inspector* with Ian and it was tremendous working with him. He was simply hilarious – my husband [actor John Turner] always says that Ian's performance in *The Government Inspector* was one of the funniest he has ever seen in his life.

The last time I worked with him was in 2004 at the Gielgud Theatre, in the Centenary Tribute to Gielgud. We did a scene from *Measure for Measure* – we'd both done it at the RSC at different times. I was in the 1950 performance with John Gielgud. I was Isabella to his Angelo and in 1970 Ian performed it with Estelle Kohler as his Isabella.

In spite of his austerity as a person he was the most amazing comic character and he was a consummate professional in all that he did. I had nothing but admiration for everything I watched him in.

Maree Wilson – Admirer and Friend

I was very young when I first saw Ian Richardson on stage in *Richard II* in Stratford, but I always remember that wonderful, singular voice.

In 1979, when I was 18, I spent most of my earnings on theatre-going. I was really excited when The Old Vic Theatre Company announced that Ian was going to be appearing in two productions, *Romeo and Juliet* and *The Government Inspector*. This was at a time when most of the country was wondering who the 'mole' was in John Le Carré's *Tinker Tailor Soldier Spy*.

I loved the *Romeo and Juliet* production but was a little disappointed that Ian wasn't there to take his curtain call. I went around to the stage door where I was informed, that 'Mr Richardson had left early' (Mercutio is killed early on in the play.) Later that week I went to see him in *The Government Inspector* – what a performance!

The pace of the whole show was just breathtaking and as the critics rightly said, Ian's performance was a *tour de force*. I went around to the stage door and there was quite a crowd. Ian couldn't have been more obliging and charming, signing autographs and chatting to everyone. I was so thrilled to meet him for the first time and mentioned that I had seen his performance in *Romeo and Juliet*, to which he replied, "Oh, yes, I'm allowed home early in that."

Little did I realise that it would be 16 years before he appeared again on stage in this country and I would next encounter him.

5

Schulz, Sherlock and Stevenson

Schulz et al.

"Richardson's portrayal of a thick-headed German officer who imagines himself to be a genius is a beautifully judged piece of acting which will surely win him an award before the year is out." The words of critic David Wheeler were extremely accurate. Appearing in *Private Schulz* in 1980, Ian won the Royal Television Society Award for Best Performance.

Ian was asked to play Major Neuheim, a pompous, bungling SS counterintelligence officer, in Jack Pulman's comedy drama. The programme was directed by Robert Chetwyn, produced by Philip Hinchcliffe and starred Michael Elphick in the title role.

Private Schulz told the story of how the Nazis came up with a scheme to forge British five pound notes and flood the UK with them, thus destabilising the economy. Schulz was a lowly petty criminal conscripted into the German army. He was meant to have ended up in Postal Censorship, but found his way into Nazi counter-intelligence because of his flair for languages and abilities as a forger.

He was given the job of clerk to Neuheim and came up with ideas for him, including the forgery scheme, for which Neuheim always took the credit. The operation to develop and print the forged notes was set up in the barracks of a concentration camp.

Many of the forgers used were Jews taken from prisons and

camps. Although *Private Schulz* was written by a Jew, there was understandably great concern not to cause offence. Schulz's main helper, Solly, was played by Cyril Shaps, himself Jewish. Both Ian and Michael Elphick often consulted Cyril Shaps to make sure that the chances of getting things wrong were minimised.

Ian actually ended up playing four roles in the series, including an uncouth Glaswegian crook, straight out of prison:

> "I played the double spy in episode three and a steward in the very last scene, but more particularly, Stanley Kemp in episode six. Philip Hinchliffe, the producer of the series said, 'Good God, you're not going to ask Richardson to play a little Glaswegian crook? He couldn't possibly do it – he's much too posh.' The director, who was more aware of my background than the producer said, 'Why don't you just give it a turn?'

> So I played Stanley and I said to Maroussia, 'I would like as part of my costume when I come out of prison, a muffler.' And she said, 'I could knit you one.' I told her it would have to be in the colours of Celtic Football Team. She knitted me a Celtic scarf, which features largely as Stanley's accoutrement. And you know, my father was still alive when *Private Schulz* went out and he said to me, 'Oh man, you were grand in *Private Schulz*, but what I will always remember as the zenith of your acting career was Stanley in the sixth episode.' And I thought, God, I've played Hamlet, Richard II, Coriolanus – I've done all these parts and my father said the zenith of my career was playing a little Glaswegian crook."

As well as the RTS award for Ian, the series won a BAFTA nomination for best serial.

David Wheeler, *The Listener*, 14 May 1981, commented: "Pulman, whom I had not previously associated with this genre, has turned in the sharpest and funniest piece of comic writing I have seen for a very long time. It is directed by Robert Chetwyn at just the right distance from realism and contains a good performance by Michael Elphick as Schulz, the petty criminal brought into the SS to run its forgery business and a quite outstanding one from Ian Richardson as Major Neuheim, the head of counter-espionage."

W. Stephen Gilbert, writing in *Broadcast* on 8 June, 1981 said: "The awards will go to Ian Richardson, exquisitely comic in the Alec Guinness dual role [this must have been written before the final episode when Ian played two further parts] of the vainglorious Major Neuheim and his alter ego, the English agent Pinkie Melford. Neuheim is one of the great television creations, the last word on misguided authority with all its unique logic, but reaction and impatience with reason... Richardson plays it absolutely for real so that his cry to the money forgers, 'Forge ahead!' and his scream at Schulz, 'All you've ever thought about is lining your own pockets', while pointing a finger wilting with flashy rings, make you explode with laughter."

Philip Hinchcliffe – Producer

I first encountered Ian in *Private Schulz* because of Robert Chetwyn. I had been asked to produce the series from scripts written by the late Jack Pulman. Bob came on board as director and we began casting. I suggested Michael Elphick for Schulz because I had seen him give a wonderful performance in Jack Rosenthal's *The Knowledge,* opposite Nigel Hawthorne; but we were scratching our heads over who could play Neuheim. It needed an actor with great attack and consummate comedic talents, but not in a sitcom way.

We were quite worried about getting the tone of the drama right – it did feature Nazis and concentration camps after all.

Robert Chetwyn – Director

Private Schulz was written by Jack Pulman. Unfortunately, he died before anyone had read the script so when I got it from the BBC I couldn't ask him about anything. Schulz was described as a very small man and Neuheim was a big man and the more I tried to cast it that way the more difficult it got and I suddenly thought it didn't really matter so much and changed it around.

I found it very difficult to find someone to play Neuheim and I was racking my brains about it. What came to me in the end was seeing Ian as Frank Ford in *The Merry Wives of Windsor* for the RSC and I thought he would be good.

Philip Hinchcliffe – Producer

At lunch one day we were going over our unimpressive list yet again when Bob's eyes suddenly lit up. He remembered a performance of Ford in *The Merry Wives of Windsor* which had brought the house down, and he thought it had been Ian in the role.

We left lunch uneaten and hared back to the office. Yes – it was Ian – and the rest as they say, is history. Ian embraced the role with open arms and immediately understood what we were trying to do with it. At the time he was not really known on television, but his success in *Private Schulz* then led on to *House of Cards*, also produced out of BBC Drama Series and he became widely recognised.

Robert Chetwyn – Director

Ian happened to be in America when I went over to find suitable Newsreel footage, which I'd decided to add to Jack's script. The national military film files were in Washington and that's where I met him. He loved the script and that was great news – I thought that he and Michael Elphick would be a very good team together.

Neuheim was only in four episodes and I felt that was a great pity because Ian was such a terrific actor. I suddenly thought – I don't know where the idea came from – that he could play the person that Schulz was having to deal with – the enemy – in every episode, whether it was Neuheim or not. First, I had to get Philip Hinchliffe to agree and he thought it was absolutely crazy, but said 'yes' in the end and Ian just loved the idea. And so Ian had to play the spy in England in the third episode and then the Scots criminal in the last one, as well as a ferry steward in the very last scene.

Philip Hinchcliffe – Producer

As the production came together, Bob and I also had to decide on two small but important roles, Pinkie Melford, a dubious British agent, and in the last episode, Stanley Kemp, a petty con. The problem was to attract good enough actors for what were minor roles. When Bob came into my office with the proposition that Ian play both roles. I was sceptical but Ian showed me how he would portray Stanley as a low life Glaswegian thug. He was hilarious and utterly convincing. So, with the help of makeup and wigs, Ian pulled off both extra parts brilliantly.

Robert Chetwyn – Director

Ian was delighted about the Scottish character because he'd never been asked to play a role like that and also because he was a Scot. He had always played upper class roles before and had never had the chance to play a common criminal.

What was very interesting about it was that absolutely nobody at all – not a critic nor a newspaper, nor a gossip columnist or even friends noticed that Ian played those four different roles. It was quite extraordinary. It had never been done on television before – at least not in that way. I was expecting the Heads of the BBC to get a bit uptight about it but nobody ever questioned it at all. The series was repeated twice over a few months and people had plenty of time to notice it but they didn't.

It was so much more effective to keep the same actor working with Michael Elphick because they worked so well together. I thought it strengthened the whole series and the casting made sense rather than dissipating it when Schulz first went to England and then again at the end. By having Ian there the whole time in four very different parts, it helped solidify the whole thing.

Ian was such a good comic actor. The reason I remembered his Ford so clearly was because I don't think I've ever seen an actor being so brilliantly funny whilst being incredibly angry. Neuheim was completely different but I thought that if this actor could make being enormously angry and jealous so funny that was exactly what I wanted for Neuheim. He was absolutely wonderful and responded superbly to it. I think at that stage he had only done mainly Shakespeare as a star actor.

I thought he was tremendously convincing in all the

roles. And of course the story was farce and worked so well because Elphick's character was so underplayed. He was the bigger man but was dominated by Ian's characters which were overplayed and that was just right.

Ian brought such an incredibly powerful performance to the series. The problem with the whole piece was trying to make the German Reich like a 'Carry On' film, without ever forgetting the truth about it, but that's really what it was. And trying to make Neuheim, an SS commander, hysterically funny, you actually quite liked him because he was so comical. But you had to balance that. Elphick's character was so sympathetic that you didn't think it was distasteful because you were with Schulz and Neuheim was the villain. And that's why it worked with Ian being Schulz's nemesis in all six episodes.

He was so inventive in his characterisation of Stan, the Scottish criminal. He saw immediately how to portray him. He was only contracted to play Neuheim and we'd actually recorded the first episode before I asked him to play the other characters and he absolutely leapt at it. I can remember having make-up and wig discussions and I was terribly impressed because he always knew just what was right for each part.

Philip Hinchcliffe – Producer

Ian was such a vital, alive, energetic person, with a love of life and a passion for acting and he was a joy to work with. He was great fun. His comic timing was unequalled. He was professional to his fingertips, but in a good way – always word perfect, incredibly well prepared and always looking for improvements in his performance right up to and during shooting.

Some actors, between takes, do the crossword or read a book or gossip with their fellow actors. Ian was always companionable, funny, approachable and responsive, but he also gave the impression that his mind was constantly at work, refining and honing the role. He had a twinkle behind the eyes which belied a very alert and curious intellect and he was an entertaining conversationalist, as many people discovered.

"The Game is Afoot"

Ian was signed up to play Sherlock Holmes in the early eighties. It was a role he was happy to be playing, but he was acutely aware that he was following in the footsteps of many acclaimed actors, notably Basil Rathbone, and that there would be much to live up to. Although several films were planned, only *The Sign of Four* and *The Hound of the Baskervilles* were made.

Desmond Davis – Director, *The Sign of Four*

The picture we have of Sherlock Holmes owes much to Sydney Paget, who in 1981 illustrated Conan Doyle's hero for the serials published in the Strand Magazine. Thus, there is the unsmiling, pale, hawk-like face, the hint of misogyny and high purpose and the dark suits topped by a deerstalker adding a welcome dash of eccentricity.

When we started rehearsals for *The Sign of Four* in 1982, Ian Richardson arrived in the rehearsal room *fait accompli*. His characterisation of the great detective was already fully formed and his lines committed to memory. Ian's Sherlock Holmes, pulsing with energy, his face wreathed in smiles, suggested a man revelling in his superior intellect who could scarcely contain himself, waiting for the next challenge to commence. 'The game is afoot!' – and what fun the game is. This was a far cry from the traditional Holmes we have come to expect – like an old friend entering the room.

I had worked with Ian once before, at the BBC, on the Solzenitsyn story *Russian Night*, and had come to appreciate his prodigious accomplishments as an actor. But his Holmes took me by surprise on that first rehearsal day. Now there is one thing that you have to learn as a director or you are in for some pretty hard lessons. That is, that on occasion it is better to keep your mouth shut. When and when not to give notes is a matter of fine judgement. If an actor is doing great things and showing you how the part can be played, however different from your own initial vision, if it is viable, go with it. Let him or her take the lead. Hang on to that old engineer's maxim, 'If it isn't broken, don't mend it'.

We got to the end of that first rehearsal scene and Ian turned to me with a quizzical, not to mention mischievous smile on his face.

I just said, "Fantastic, Ian."

Terence Rigby – Inspector Layton, *The Sign of Four*

This was a film intended as one of a package of about seven starring Ian as Sherlock. It was soon clear that there were many intrigues going on in the background – updates of which were given one at ungodly hours in the mornings by the drivers, who carried the cast into Shepperton. On a film, the drivers 'know everything' –

it is a fact. A couple of the technical staff were the first to go – then the unthinkable: Trevor Howard, one of the greatest of names in film, who had been due to play a small cameo role, was 'removed' and replaced. I feel sure he never made another picture.

Then the focus was switched as to whether David Healey as Dr Watson would be engaged for the remaining stories. Several of the cast were up in arms, keen to do an Equity 'mutiny'. Ian remained calm as ever, refraining from being drawn to definitive action of such a 'revolutionary' nature, even though aware of the pressure.

I was playing Lestrade – a famous Holmes character who appeared in many of the stories. My name was changed to Layton, thus avoiding my further inclusion. The last curio we heard as we were gradually coming to the end of our various stints on the film, was that the voice of the unmatchable Ian was to be dubbed – because of his English sound. Happily, this was never to come to fruition.

I recall being deeply moved while we were rehearsing a scene together, when Ian halted the director, Des Davies, and the scene, to say how refreshing it was to have me in the drama – for my immense 'reality', which helped him personally to find the true and accurate balance of his portrayal of Sherlock. Thank you, dearest Ian – I was quite gob-smacked.

Brian Blessed – Geoffrey Lyons, *The Hound of the Baskervilles*

In *The Hound of the Baskervilles*, they were trying to find locations in Surrey, which is where I live, and I found a couple. Ian was thrilled to bits that I went out of my way to show them woods and walks where they could film – because by then I'd finished my filming.

There was one scene in which my character breaks down and cries because he thinks he has killed his wife. Ian had never seen me cry as an actor and he was absolutely distraught watching the scene in the studio. They couldn't film for a couple of hours, as they had to adjust his make-up because he had cried so much.

I think that he was one of the best Sherlock Holmes I've ever seen – I'd rank him alongside Jeremy Brett. Ian was the best for subtlety and I thought he got the character perfectly. Every scene, every expression he had worked on – there wasn't a lazy bone in his body. Everything was keenly observed from the book because he felt a tremendous sense of obligation and total devotion to getting it right for Conan Doyle. I remember him saying to me, "When I die, I might meet Arthur Conan Doyle and I want to be able to face him and say with total integrity that I did my best as Sherlock Holmes."

His Holmes knew exactly who he was and because of it had a certain threatening physical power in a strange, subtle way. You felt that underneath the costume, Ian was made of steel and it was an amazingly observed performance.

David Stuart Davies – Writer and Sherlockian authority

I seem to have been writing about Sherlock Holmes – and particularly the dramatic presentations of the character – since the dawn of time. Well, most of my life, at least. It does mean that I have had the pleasure and privilege of meeting many of the actors who have played the great detective, including the charmingly genteel Peter Cushing, the brilliantly eccentric Jeremy Brett and the generous and witty Ian Richardson.

Ian gave a very considered and spirited portrayal of Holmes, combining perfectly the detective's cerebral qualities with his heroic dimensions. He also managed to inject humour and warmth into the relationship with Watson – so often missing in other versions.

I first contacted him in 1997 through his agent, with a request to interview him about the two Holmes movies he made for television in the 1980s. Ian invited me to his dressing room at the Strand Theatre, where he was appearing in Pinero's *The Magistrate*, warning me in a letter that he recalled very little of the films. As it turned out he recalled nearly everything. He welcomed me warmly, made me feel at ease straight away and then launched into a series of tales full of naughty gossip about the two productions.

So caught up was he in his recital that he seemed not to notice that the clock was ticking towards seven-thirty and curtain up. When I pointed this out, Ian appeared not in the least perturbed and insisted on finishing his final anecdote.

The two Holmes films, *The Hound of the Baskervilles* and *The Sign of Four*, were filmed in 1982. American producer Sy Weintraub had been successfully producing *Tarzan* adventures for television in the Seventies, but as that decade grew to a close he began a search for a new character to turn into a television star. He chose Sherlock Holmes.

Unfortunately, Weintraub was unaware that the copyright on the Holmes stories was about to expire in

England and he went through a great deal of unnecessary legal wrangling with the Conan Doyle estate in order to gain permission to use them. He was also unaware of Granada Television's plans to film a Sherlock series once the stories came into public domain at the end of 1980 — fifty years after Doyle's death.

Blissfully ignorant of this threat to his venture, Weintraub came to England to look for his Holmes. He engaged a producer named Otto Plaschkes, who by chance happened to see Ian on television. Ian said that he was appearing in:

"A terrible little detective thing that I did called *A Cotswold Death*, playing a police inspector [Anthony Arrowsmith] who in the course of his duty attempted to emulate the methods of Sherlock Holmes.

Plaschkes turned to his wife Louise and said, 'That's our Holmes.'"

Ian told me what happened next:

"I went along to be interviewed for the part and they were slightly dismayed that I was only five foot ten. I explained that in *A Cotswold Death* I had worn lifts. Anyway, Weintraub liked me and he signed me up for six films."

In preparation for the series, Ian read all the stories, annotating them in order to create a detailed file on all aspects of the detective's life: his habits, moods, sayings, clothes, etc:

"It was my Holmes Bible and I became a walking encyclopaedia of Sherlock."

The first film to be shot was *The Sign of Four*, in the late summer of 1982, followed by *The Hound of the*

Baskervilles. Halfway through the shooting of the second feature, the news broke that Granada was going to do all the Sherlock Holmes stories with Jeremy Brett. Ian recalled that Weintraub was furious because he'd paid a lot of money to obtain permission from the Doyle estate and here was Granada waltzing in to steal his thunder.

Weintraub took them to court. According to Ian, the producer had a very good case, but eventually there was an out of court settlement for a huge sum of money, which was enough for Weintraub to cover his costs on both *The Sign* and *The Hound* and make a profit, too. And so the producer took the money and wrapped up his Holmes project after just two movies.

Ian had mixed feelings about the early termination of his Holmes career:

"In an odd sort of way, I heaved a sigh of relief. That was because I didn't want to get too associated with Sherlock Holmes. I felt that Jeremy [Brett] — such a nice man — towards the end rather regretted it. And I lost out on playing the emperor in the film *Amadeus* [1984; Jeffrey Jones got the part] because Weintraub wouldn't let me go while the court case was pending. This upset me terribly."

There was another reason for Ian's relief at not making more of the movies:

"I had to battle all the time to keep things true to the character and the books. The writer was Charles Edward Pogue - very American. And the writing was very American. There were phrases and actions in the films that no English writer worth his salt would have countenanced. I spent a great deal of time Anglicising my text to make it sound like Conan Doyle and I was also able to put them right on a few inaccuracies.

However I couldn't, unfortunately, budge them and prevent them from spending £10,000 on top of the budget to build a separate bedroom to show that Watson actually occupied a different room from Holmes' bedroom to avoid any suggestion... (Ian gave a downward wave of the hand). I said to them, 'What are you worried about?'"

Similarly, Weintraub and Plaschkes had puritanical views on Holmes' cocaine habit:

"I wanted to do more of the drug thing, but they wouldn't have it. I thought this was important because, in a curious way, this one area of human weakness humanises an otherwise inhuman computer-type of man.

They did allow me to smoke a lot, but I had to bow to the American request to smoke a Meerschaum. Weintraub said, 'This is the image of Sherlock Holmes.' But I pointed out that he smoked all sorts of pipes – briars, clays – but not a monstrosity like a Meerschaum. Sy just hooded his eyes and said, 'You will smoke a Meerschaum.' It was all part of the attitude on the set – a kind of, 'what does it matter? Who will notice?' attitude."

In the early 1980's, Ian was extremely busy, playing a variety of parts. He was the eccentric hypochondriac, Frederick Fairlie in a superb adaptation of Wilkie Collins' *The Woman in White* – a role he was to reprise in 1997. Fellow performers included Diana Quick, Jenny Seagrove, John Shrapnel and Alan Badel, in one of his final roles, as Count Fosco.

He took the role of James Ramsay MacDonald, the first British Labour prime minister and fellow Scot, in *Underdog*, as part of the *Number 10* series on British leaders.

Another part he played was Adrien Avigdor, a Jewish art dealer, in the mini series *Mistral's Daughter*, which starred Stacy Keach, Stephanie Powers and Lee Remick.

Stacy Keach – actor, Julien Mistral

My first experience of Ian Richardson was as a member of the audience at the Royal Shakespeare Company's Aldwych Theatre in London in 1965, at Peter Brook's legendary production of *Marat/Sade*. He was playing Jean-Paul Marat and as a young aspiring actor, I was immediately taken by his extraordinary ability to convey complicated emotional colours with amazing dexterity.

Some years later, I found myself playing the same role in a Williamstown summer stock production and I know that because Ian's performance had been so etched in my memory, I could not help but emulate many of the choices he had made. In fact, I must confess that my own personal success in the role was largely due to *his* original conception. It has been said that when you steal something from another actor, 'steal from the best' and Ian Richardson was certainly one of the best actors of his generation.

Over the years, I followed many of his numerous triumphs with joy and adulation, particularly his inimitable portrayal of Sherlock Holmes, but it wasn't until I had the pleasure and privilege of working with Ian on *Mistral's Daughter* that I began to fully appreciate the scope and breadth of his talent. Ian was a master technician with enormous sensitivity. His phraseology always seemed to reflect not only a keen intelligence, but also a deep sense of emotional vulnerability.

It was such a thrill for me to sit across the table from Ian in the scene we happened to be shooting in a beautiful villa in the south of France. I had to pinch myself a couple of times. I could hardly believe that I was actually working with one of my acting heroes.

Private Schulz with Michael Elphick

As Stanley Kemp - one of four roles Ian played in *Private Schulz*

Ian as Nehru, with Sam Dastor, Indian President Zail Singh, Janet Suzman and Nicol Williamson

Ian and Napoleon

Lord Groan in *Gormenghast*

The Author with Ian on location at Pollok House for *The Dark Beginnings of Sherlock Holmes*

Becoming an Honorary Doctor of Drama at the Royal Scottish Academy of Music and Drama, 1999

On the makeup bus with John Sessions and makeup designer Meg Spiers, for *Murder Rooms*

With Judi Dench and Bill Nighy in Winchester, 2003
Photo © Joan Street

Maroussia, Judi Dench and Ian in Winchester, 2003
Photo © Joan Street

Ian in Edinburgh

Cutting a dash as Doctor Joseph Bell

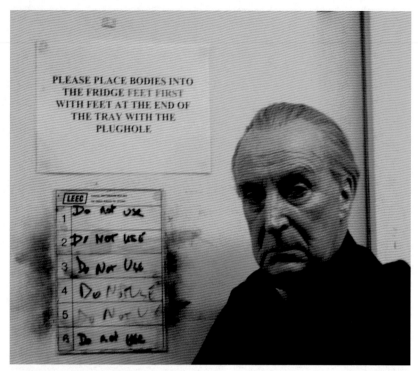

As the sinister Canon Black, in *Strange*

Ian and Maroussia, Devon, April 2004

Ian at his Devon home, April 2004

In the garden, Devon, April 2004

Creeper Boys – Ian with Oliver Dimsdale (left) and Alan Cox, in Windsor

Relaxing between performances
at the National Theatre,
September 2006

University of Stirling, 2006 – receiving an
Honorary Doctorate from the Chancellor,
Diana Rigg

With Lesley Manville in *The Alchemist*
© Stephen Commiskey, National Theatre

As the shooting progressed, I also had the pleasure of getting to know Ian personally. He was such a gracious and giving soul, possessed of a delicious sense of humour – who could forget his 'Grey Poupon mustard commercials' – and he was always totally professional in his distinguished demeanour.

[In these commercials, which were hugely successful in the States, Ian is in a Rolls Royce which pulls up beside another Rolls in which Paul Eddington is sitting, eating. Ian says, "Pardon me. Would you have any Grey Poupon?" To many Americans, Ian is still 'the guy from the Grey Poupon commercial'].

He was a shining example of what it means to be an actor of respectability. I consider myself blessed to have been able to work with him and I shall always be grateful to him for giving us so many indelibly memorable moments through his extraordinary talent and his enduring charm.

The Master of Ballantrae

Ian played Mr MacKellar, the prim but devoted steward to the estate of Lord Durisdeer, in the HTV dramatisation of the Robert Louis Stevenson classic, *The Master of Ballantrae*, made in 1983. It gave him the opportunity to work with John Gielgud, whom he had first encountered at the RSC and who was one of the actors he admired most:

"*Ballantrae* was made in England at the house of Jane Seymour. It was the last time I worked with John Gielgud, who was playing the Master. I remember he played a death scene in it and he was lying on a slab out on the courtyard and I said to him, 'Are you quite comfortable, John?' and he said to me, 'I'm just rehearsing for the real thing.' Thankfully it was not to happen for another twenty years.

73

What was nice, was that the dialogue coach on it because not only did we have British, but American actors was Iain Cuthbertson, who had been a colleague of mine in Glasgow and who indeed used to lecture on the poems of Robert Burns. He married my leading lady from my years there who, as she was then known, was Anne Byers. She died sadly young of the dreaded 'C'. Iain was my sponsor the day the RSAMD decided to honour me with a Doctorate in Drama. Wheels come full circle."

—◆◆◆—

Nickolas Grace – Dass

After the Old Vic Company, we worked together again in *The Master of Ballantrae*, with John Gielgud, Timothy Dalton, Richard Thomas and Michael York amongst others. Ian and Gielgud seemed to have a close bond. There were some marvellous cake shops round where we were filming. Ian and I used to go with one of the other actors, whose wife found out and banned him. But Ian and I kept getting them and we'd share them out in the Winnebago.

6

Becoming Nehru and a Commander

Mountbatten: The Last Viceroy

In 1985, a badly photocopied photo led to Ian landing the role of Nehru in the drama series *Mountbatten: The Last Viceroy*. He had hoped to play Mountbatten but he had neither the height nor the physical appearance to portray Lord Louis. However, producer Judith de Paul was having great difficulty casting an actor to play India's first prime minister until she stumbled across the photocopy. Covering over the top half of Ian's head, she noticed a strong resemblance to Jawaharlal Nehru.

The series portrayed Mountbatten's time as the last Viceroy of India and then the first Governor-General, post-independence. It was well known that Mountbatten's wife, Edwina, and Nehru were extremely close and probably lovers but in order to maintain the support and assistance of the Indian government the relationship could only be hinted at in the drama.

As Ian recalled, playing Nehru was a very special experience for him:

> "I loved filming in India, because I was actually expected to play an Asian and it was necessary for me to absorb as much of that temperament as was available to me. That comes not just from mingling with the people and their

slight idiosyncrasies and the way they talk and things like that, but to become of aware of the climate they live in and how that affects them. And that was rather special for me, because I love them, I adore them and so consequently when I come across Indians I feel a great affinity towards them.

India is endlessly ancient and the music and the vibrations that you feel off the streets and the smells – it's incredibly old and magical and it can affect you. Some people I know hate it, not for us though.

We were within one week of finishing the filming in India of Mountbatten, who was the last Viceroy. The Premier of India was the daughter of Pandit Nehru, whom I played. In the film, I was covered in olive-coloured makeup and wore brown contact lenses. It was thought that it might be a nice idea for me to meet Mrs Gandhi. Not just me, but all the principal performers of the piece. The meeting took place in the garden of the house, on the spot where a couple of weeks later she was gunned down. And I think that was probably the most memorable meeting of my career.

I was anxious about meeting her but she was enchanting to me. I said to her, "Madam, I'm acutely nervous meeting you," and she said, "Why?" I responded, "Well, I believe you had to look at a photograph of my interpretation of your illustrious father." She said that she was very proud. She was very nice and I remember that she spoke very quietly.

She was wearing her accustomed sari, and I looked down at her hands, preparatory to seeing whether she wanted to shake my hand or not. I noticed that they were clasped and her knuckles were white. Even then, so soon before she was assassinated, she was aware that her life was in jeopardy. I'll never forget that."

Ian's performance was highly praised. Philip Purser, in the obituary he wrote in *The Guardian* on 10 February, 2007, said that he made Nehru, "the most mercurial character in the drama." Howard Rosenberg, *Los Angeles Times*, 24 January, 1986, describing Ian's performance as "stunning", added, "Richardson is one of Britain's most versatile actors, a man of infinite faces and personalities, this time triumphing as the outwardly charming, inwardly tough Nehru."

Sam Dastor – Actor, Mahatma Gandhi

The filming of *Mountbatten* took almost five and a half months and Ian and I were, I think, the only ones who were there from Day One to the very end. I worked very closely with him and it was a joy to do so.

We filmed for two months in the UK, mostly in Luton Hoo and then in Delhi and environs for ten weeks. We had been given permission by Mrs Gandhi to film everything we wanted in India except for the scenes of Hindu-Muslim violence which took place immediately after Independence, so we scheduled those for filming in Sri Lanka for two weeks after Delhi. In the event it was ironic that Mrs Gandhi was assassinated on Wednesday 30 October – we had finished our filming the afternoon before – and we then witnessed the most terrible scenes of Hindu-Sikh violence in Delhi, before going to Sri Lanka to film the 1948 scenes of Hindu-Muslim violence. It was surreal in a way.

Actually Delhi was bedlam in the few days after the assassination and all flights in and out were suspended whilst the world and his wife arrived for the funeral (by which I mean Mrs Thatcher, Mitterand etc). Most of the cast had left for four days of sightseeing but Ian and I had both stayed in Delhi.

It was so hard to get a flight. The England cricket team had just arrived to start a Test series against India which had to be cancelled. The Prime Minister of Sri Lanka who was over for the funeral invited the English team to come over to Colombo and play there instead and offered them a flight on his personal jet. They were all staying in the same hotel as us so we heard about this at first hand. There were also lots of Western journalists there covering the cricket who wanted to go to Sri Lanka but couldn't get a flight, so our producer, Judith de Paul, offered to take them on our chartered flight on Sunday which we did (about 60 of them in all as I remember).

Nicol Williamson and Janet Suzman had finished filming and went back to the UK but Ian and I went on to Candy via Colombo and it is there that I have the most vivid and happiest memories of Ian and Maroussia. We had plenty of free time so we hired a chauffeur-driven car and went all around the great archaeological sites of Sri Lanka, Anuradhapura, Polonnoruwa and the Lion Rock of Sigiriya.

It's difficult to summarise Ian's performance as Nehru. What I would say is that he bore a remarkable facial likeness to him and his naturally crisp delivery of lines was ideally suited to Nehru's 'more British than the British' tones. Ian always maintained that Nehru must have modelled his speeches on those of Churchill. I could never see that myself, though he might have been right (they were both, after all, old Harrovians) but I loved hearing Ian expound his theory, which he did often and very enthusiastically!

Janet Suzman – Actress, Edwina Mountbatten

Ian's uncanny resemblance to Nehru when made up

and dressed was almost unnerving. So much so that he managed to quieten the very understandable resentment felt by many in the Indian cast, who naturally wanted one of their number to play such an important figure. (The justifying logic was further underlined by the fact that [Polish-born] Vladek Shaybal was cast as Jinnah – an almost equally important character.)

Ian and I were constantly intrigued by the rumours circulating non-stop about the reputed affair that Edwina and Nehru were said to have embarked on.

One day we were filming a scene where the two of them were walking through an arbor in the Vice-Regal gardens and an *old party* in a green sari bustled up to us as we were waiting for a line-up, Ian's arm about my waist. She moved his arm slightly lower so that his hand rested on my butt and grinned widely and said, "That's where his hand would always be," before bustling off again. Maybe it was – maybe it wasn't, but we both liked it and kept it for the shot.

We also agreed with the producer to film an extra scene showing the two of them embracing in Nehru's rooms at Government House, but it was (I think rightly) cut from the final version as being too explicit. Subtlety was the order of the day and Ian was a master of that.

Enough will be said about his class as an actor, his Samurai-edged English, his baleful eye, his exquisite timing and his voice, which could have made him an operatic tenor of the first rank were he not doomed to the ineffable glories of Shakespearian verse. I admired his acting without reserve – from my first taste of it in that ever-green *The Comedy of Errors* way back in our youth – right through to watching him do his stuff in

The Hollow Crown every night for many, many weeks. He was as funny, as cutting, as darkly melancholic and as inventive on the first as he was on the last performance.

Suffice it to say, he was my idea of the 'Great British Actor.'

———◆———

Troubles

In *Troubles* (1988), set just after the First World War, Ian played the eccentric Edward Spencer, owner of the rundown Majestic Hotel in rural Ireland. Amongst other cast members were Ian Charleson, Emer Gillespie, Sean Bean and James Ellis.

———◆———

Susannah Harker – Actress, Angela Spencer

The first time I met Ian was on *Troubles*, which was filmed in Ireland. I was only 23 at the time and it was about my second filming job. Christopher Morahan was the director – wonderful, but he was quite a force and quite formidable.

They were nearly halfway through shooting when I began my scenes. I remember wandering round this enormous mansion which was almost like a castle. I found myself in costume in the middle of this huge drawing room, not really knowing what to do with myself.

The doors burst open and in came this force of nature, Ian Richardson – in these long boots. He was looking very impressive and he was smoking a cigarette, which he often did, though he denied it. He was very loud and absolutely furious with someone and swearing like a trooper. And he just said to me, "You're on, you're on – they don't tell you anything here!" He was in an absolute frenzy. He told me he had to go on and then I had to walk through the French windows onto the lawn and I thought, well I had better.

He wandered off and that was my introduction to him, when he was in real dudgeon – it was very funny.

—◆◆◆—

Porterhouse Blue

In Malcolm Bradbury's adaptation of Tom Sharpe's hilarious novel, *Porterhouse Blue*, set in a fictional Cambridge college, Ian played Sir Godber Evans, the new liberal, reforming Master. The college traditionalists were appalled by his attempts to bring the institution into the 20th century, none more so than the Head Porter Scullion, played by David Jason, and the senior tutor played by Ian's former RSC colleague, Paul Rogers. Also appearing in the drama as an undergraduate was Ian's son, Miles, whose character Gimingham heckles the Master at the college feast and describes him as, 'a perverted little man.'

—◆◆◆—

Barbara Jefford – Lady Mary Evans

I worked with Ian in *Porterhouse Blue,* when we played husband and wife. I remember the director, Robert Knights, always called Ian 'Sir'. He was so incredibly funny as Godber Evans, the Master.

—◆◆◆—

John Sessions – actor, Lionel Zipser

I was really thrilled to be working with Ian in *Porterhouse* and with David Jason and so many others like Paul Rogers and Ian Wallace. I felt very much like the boy even though I was 33. I was quite scared of meeting Ian because his demeanour, as I understood it, was quite fierce, but he was terribly sweet to me and very kind. I was also impressed very early on how close Ian and Maroussia were – they were just inseparable.

I remember when we were doing *Porterhouse*, it was about the time that *nouvelle cuisine* came in and it absolutely incensed Ian. He said to me, "You pay £25 and you get a carrot and a spiral of gravy round a plate. I will not pay that kind of money for an edible picture."

I was to do a show about Napoleon the following year. Ian, who had played Marat in the *Marat/Sade*, had a keen interest in Napoleon. He had me round for supper in his house in London one evening and lent me some books, bless his heart, on the Emperor and gave me some Napoleonic egg cups, which I still have.

I said to him that I'd love him to come and see the show and he responded, "You know, John, I'm afraid I won't, because I might not like it and I'd have to tell you." And I loved him for that – he was so direct and his standards are *the* standards. He was my childhood hero and I'd grown up with all those wonderful performances at the RSC. Getting to know and working with Ian was an absolute honour.

There were many other performances by Ian in the second half of the 1980's. Amongst the films he took part in were *Brazil,*

Whoops Apocalypse, *The Fourth Protocol* (alongside Michael Caine), *Cry Freedom* and *Burning Secret*, in which he played Faye Dunaway's husband.

In television he was also busy, playing the title role in *Blunt*, about Sir Anthony Blunt and the Cambridge Spies. He got the chance to work opposite Sir Alec Guinness again in *Monsignor Quixote*. Other sublime roles were the director Ray Malcolm in Noel Coward's *Star Quality* and an eye-catching performance as 'Gentlemanly Johnny' General Burgoyne in Bernard Shaw's *The Devil's Disciple*.

In the 1989 Queen's Birthday Honours' List, Ian was made a Commander of the Order of the British Empire [CBE]. Maroussia, Jeremy and Miles joined him at the Palace and Ian was grateful that his extremely proud father, who died not long afterwards, got the chance to see his medal.

7

Putting a Bit of Stick About – the Francis Urquhart Years

In 1990, Ian was relaxing at the house in the South of France in which Maroussia had been born and which she had inherited from her family, when a large package was delivered to him.

As soon as he read the first few pages of the *House of Cards* scripts, he knew that the role of Francis Urquhart had to be his. He called his agent, Jean Diamond, straight away and told her that he wanted the part:

> "From the moment I read the first scripts, I felt that not only was it the biggest acting opportunity to come my way since my Shakespeare days, but probably was going to be something rather special on the box.
>
> It was very odd, because we took a wee while to film it, as by this time we'd abandoned going into a studio in White City on six moveable cameras over two days. By then we used to go out with a 16mm camera and film it like you film a movie and I can remember that nobody ever said from one day to the next, boy, are we sitting on something special, but the atmosphere was such at the end of the day's filming that I got into the car and said to the chauffeur, 'My, today was just wild,' and he said, 'I

think you're on a winner,' but nobody else would.

And of course it was a winner. It just cleaned up every award that was going."

Although he shared Ian's beautiful manners, Urquhart was otherwise the antithesis of his persona, as he was at pains to point out:

"Francis Urquhart was not my friend and I did not enjoy living his life. I used to hate my face in the shaving mirror in the morning because it was the face of Francis Urquhart. But, it has to be said that rather like Richard III is the great Shakespearian opportunity of a lifetime, so in terms of my television career, Urquhart was my biggest opportunity. Nobody knew who the hell I was and I was never recognised on any street until I played him."

'FU', as he became known, became the character everyone was talking about in the early '90's. Despite his villainous deeds, the way he drew his audience in and almost made them feel like co-conspirators added to Urquhart's appeal. And there was a great deal of female attention because of the power and personal magnetism Ian brought to the character:

"That kind of power is in itself a sort of aphrodisiac. That this man is capable of an aura of power and has this Machiavellian deviousness about him is, I think, almost certainly sexually arousing. I have to say, personally, that being a Scottish Presbyterian, I find that really rather revolting and it used to embarrass me enormously.

I remember one time particularly, when as the result of playing Francis Urquhart I was invited to go and do a radio interview. The lady who was responsible for getting me there was quite clearly anxious that I shouldn't rush off afterwards. I didn't know where to look. I wanted to say to her, 'Look, although you've got the right idea about Francis Urquhart, you've got totally the wrong idea about me – the two of us don't blend.'"

House of Cards, adapted for television by Andrew Davies from Conservative spin doctor Michael Dobbs' novel, was broadcast in November 1990. It introduced the world to the catchphrase, 'You might very well think that; I couldn't possibly comment', which is now part of the national lexicon.

To Play the King saw Urquhart established as Prime Minister and looking for a challenge, which came in the form of the newly crowned king, played by Michael Kitchen who, seeing himself as the voice of the people, must take on Urquhart.

In *The Final Cut*, Urquhart faced his biggest battle yet – to hold onto power and beat Margaret Thatcher's record as longest-serving prime minister. Urquhart had been in power for eleven years and there were mutterings from his cabinet colleagues that he should go. There were also many ghosts from his past coming back to haunt him.

Ian was surrounded by a strong supporting cast, many of them female. In all three series his wife, Elizabeth, who would have given Lady Macbeth a run for her money, was played by Diane Fletcher. The love interest in *House of Cards* was provided by the character of Mattie Storin, a political correspondent who fell for Urquhart's potent charms, played by Susannah Harker. In *To Play the King*, Sarah Harding, played by Kitty Aldridge, became Urquhart's political advisor and eventually his lover. Clare Carlsen, Urquhart's Parliamentary Private Secretary, but this time not his lover, in *The Final Cut*, was played by Isla Blair.

Colin Jeavons played Urquhart's political sidekick, Tim Stamper in the first two series. In *The Final Cut*, Tom Makepeace, originally a member of Urquhart's Cabinet, who becomes his main challenger, was played by Paul Freeman. There was also a role for Ian's son Miles, as an army officer, though he and his father didn't have any scenes together.

Reviewing the first episode of *House of Cards* in *The Times* on 19 November 1990, Sheridan Morley said: "Urquhart-Richardson wanders around the corridors of power like some papal nuncio, bestowing blessings on those he is about to dismember. There is something about Richardson's semi-detached grandeur which makes him the perfect spy if only for himself; years of acting in Shakespeare and John Le Carré have equipped him with an elegant mix of arrogance and treachery."

Michael Dobbs – Author

I wrote *House of Cards* simply to fill in time beside a pool, with no intention of publishing it.

For it to be published and made into a series with someone like Ian just taking the role and making it his own was extraordinary. A huge amount of the success of the series was down to his portrayal of Francis Urquhart. When I first met the cast it was quite clear that it *was* him. He was very much as I had imagined 'FU' to be. And the catch phrase "You might very well think that; I couldn't possibly comment", which Andrew Davies actually came up with, was Ian's line as much as anybody's because he brought so much to it.

I feel quite embarrassed because although it was his best-known role, we tend to forget what a brilliant actor he was in so many other roles that were much greater than 'FU'.

We met several times. I remember him inviting me to lunch at the Garrick Club, in London, where he was a member. I was sitting having lunch with Ian and Maroussia and noticed the then Chancellor of the Exchequer, Kenneth Clarke, and waved to him. His eyes lit up and he came straight across the room and I thought how wonderful it was going to be to introduce my friends to the Chancellor. But he wasn't interested in talking to me – he simply wanted to meet 'Francis Urquhart', which was rather lovely.

When Ian returned to the theatre in 1995, after a long

absence, in Pinero's *The Miser*, I had dinner with him in Chichester. It was another example of what a consummate professional he was. Many people would have just wanted to milk the 'FU' role but he took a wonderfully brave and courageous decision to go back to the theatre after 14 years. He decided he wanted to remain an actor rather than a caricature.

I remember a photographer coming to visit me telling me how he had just been to photograph Ian. He said it was very eerie. There he was taking photographs of him and he asked if he could have some of Francis Urquhart. Ian looked away for a moment, composed himself and turned back and it was Urquhart. A change had come over his face and eyes.

Ken Riddington – Producer

Paul Seed and I have worked together on so many occasions, so you can imagine the thoughts that went on as to who should play the lead in *House of Cards*. I can't remember who had the idea, but we certainly got a letter from Ian's agent. I do recall that we met Ian for the first time in a hotel in Shepherd's Bush at lunchtime. Prior to this meeting, Paul and I had decided that it would be disastrous to have a leading man who was under the impression that he was more important than *House of Cards* or indeed Paul and myself.

We had also agreed that we would think about things overnight and not come to any snap decision. The following morning came and thank goodness we were both in favour – Ian would play Francis Urquhart.

Paul and I knew, some months later, that we had made the correct choice. Never once did Ian falter throughout and both he and Paul got everything just right. At the very start, the three of us had a talk and agreed as to what sort of person Urquhart should be on screen.

Ian was always kind, prompt and never ever reminded anyone that he was the star or 'God's Gift'. Never once did he throw a temper tantrum – if he thought anything was wrong he would come and talk quietly to Paul or myself.

⸻

Andrew Davies – Scriptwriter

I first saw Ian Richardson as an unforgettable Coriolanus at Stratford. I admired the steeliness of his performance, the way he could convey, simultaneously and paradoxically, terrifying strength and extreme fragility. Later, I was entranced by his performance in *Tinker Tailor Soldier Spy*.

But I was a little taken aback when he was cast as Francis Urquhart in *House of Cards*. When I was writing the scripts (ruthlessly asset-stripped from Michael Dobbs's novel) I imagined one of those big, beefy, back-slapping politicians – a great bear of a man with a hug like a polar bear. Less than five minutes into the read-through, I was seduced, to the point that I couldn't remember why I had thought of Urquhart in any other way than Ian's.

I remember in rehearsals, he was a little wary of the asides to camera at first. The prevailing wisdom was that talking to the audience was something that just didn't work in television; people thought that it destroyed the suspension of disbelief. But Ian was brilliant at it from the start. His little looks and glances were so subtle, accurate and precisely directed that I gradually wrote fewer and fewer words into these asides and simply wrote: "Urquhart gives us one of his looks." He invariably chose the right one!

He was always frighteningly well prepared – one of those exceptional actors who inspire the rest of the class to raise their game. Always impeccably courteous and thoughtful, he had ways of letting one know when his displeasure had been incurred. Usually one of his looks would do the trick.

Paul Seed – Director, *House of Cards* and *To Play the King*

The tremendous success of *House of Cards* was a complete and utter shock to us all – we knew we'd done something a bit different, a bit good and a bit cheeky, but we couldn't believe our luck at the timing of the totally unforeseen resignation of Margaret Thatcher. The transmission date of 18 November had been set in April, at a time when Margaret Thatcher had appeared utterly invulnerable. [Thatcher resigned as Prime Minister four days after the first episode was broadcast]. It was astonishing.

You just knew the frisson of shock that was going to run through all those viewers at home – nothing really to do with what we'd *done,* just *timing* and it was one of those rare, electric moments of television, like when Kenneth Tynan actually said 'fuck' on live TV at a time, in 1965, when saying 'bloody' was a bit daring.

I've never worked with anybody quite as much like a well-honed machine as Ian. He was the Rolls-Royce of actors. His precision, timing and passion for getting it 'right' were extraordinary.

Up until *House of Cards*, the aside was a largely

theatrical device confined to pantomime and the odd seventeenth century classic. Now, Andrew Davies had been encouraged by Mike Wearing (then Head of Series at the BBC) to take a 'Jacobean' approach to the adaptation of Michael Dobbs' book. Andrew had 'gone for it large' and used *Richard III* [coincidentally, the last role Ian played at the RSC] as the template for Urquhart, asides and all. Ian very quickly started to enjoy himself. He was brilliant at it and it was his precision that made it work as well as it did.

When I brought the first lot of film rushes home from shooting the Party Conference scenes down in Brighton, my partner practically jumped out of her chair when Ian turned to camera for his first aside. He was like a striking snake in the speed and accuracy of his eye contact with the camera lens, buttonholing us with Urquhart's chilling inner thoughts – as unnerving as Anthony Hopkins' jagged intakes of breath in *The Silence of the Lambs*. So many people have used the aside in TV dramas since then (not least in other Andrew Davies scripts) but there has been no-one within miles of Ian for making it really count.

His precision, dedication and attention to detail could, however, occasionally rebound on him. Prior to filming I always like to have a short period of time with the principal actors, during which we can get to know each other and achieve common agreement about character, character relationships, dialogue and development of scenes. Ian had decided many things about Urquhart and he seemed to like all my suggestions. One of the things he was most certain about was the 'old-school' core of the man and his philosophy. This would show most obviously in his manner of dress and I agreed wholeheartedly.

A specific, along with the cut of his suits, his Guards tie etc., was the wearing of starched, separate collars for his shirts. Spot-on, I thought. These were duly got and Ian looked great in them – they were absolutely right for the character. Unfortunately, those collars are by nature crisp, hard and sharp and the style Ian had chosen stood up quite high. Now he didn't have *that* many asides in the first week or so of filming and we were all delighted with the look and feel of Urquhart and very happily committed to a continuity for the series.

By the time we got up to Manchester to do the House of Commons stuff on Granada's (then) standing set, we were working with heavier and consequently *hotter* lights. Ian's make-up was thicker than it might have been under normal circumstances because he had been staying at his and Maroussia's house outside Nice for a month or so prior to filming. He'd acquired a decidedly un-Urquhart-like Mediterranean tan, which took quite a bit of covering-up to give him the desired icy Scottish pallor.

Also, the asides to camera now started coming thick and fast once we were doing the scenes on the floor of the House. The inevitable result was that poor Ian found he was rapidly becoming in danger of sawing his own head off on every turn. And it was by then too late to change the continuity of either the costume or the asides.

Interestingly, when we came to do *To Play the King*, Ian decided that Urquhart no longer wore anything but *soft* collars, probably attached to hand-made shirts. I can't quite remember what the character justification was for this but it was extremely well-argued.

Another example of his craftsmanship came during the filming of *To Play the King*. We were doing a scene at Lyme Hall just outside Manchester, one of the many locations that were used to create different areas of

Buckingham Palace. The scene was with Michael Kitchen as the king and was set in the Palace gardens. It was quite a long one and Ian had nearly, if not all, of the dialogue – long speeches with complicated argument as he tried to persuade the king to do his bidding.

It was a scene that needed to be on the move and we were working at a time when steadicam was considered to be much more of a decadent luxury than it is now. [A steadicam is a device that mechanically isolates the movement of the camera from that of the operator, providing a very smooth shot even when the cameraman is moving at speed over rough terrain.]

We ended up with a massively long track along a gravel path at the end of which we had to pan the camera right, to follow the two of them as they turned and walked away from us up a flight of steps and along another path, still deep in conversation. I was then going to move the camera in to a new position to pick them up and track ahead of them again as they came up the steps towards us.

The cameraman, the script-supervisor (continuity) and I all had slightly different opinions of exactly what Ian should be doing and saying at the point we would be picking him up for second shot – essential for us to know in order to make the cut between the two shots work accurately.

Ian, however, knew *exactly* what he was doing and saying. Despite walking and talking non-stop for several minutes prior to the moment in question he knew to the syllable of what word he was saying and which foot he was on, as he trod on the first step of the flight to the new path and the new shot. That amount of technique doesn't half make filming easier for everyone behind the camera.

Talking so much about Ian's technique risks giving the impression of an actor without much heart and soul. Nothing could be further from the truth. Technique for an actor is the same as for a musician. The ability to hit a note accurately is not what art's about – machines are at least as good at that. It has to be done, of course, but it is the *sound* and *quality* and *passion* of the note once hit that is important. Ian's technique permitted him great breadth and depth in his performance and that was its sole purpose.

He was also *huge* fun to work with. We laughed an awful lot – often too much. Ian could be a dreadful giggler and on many occasions we had to cut the camera because he was in hysterics about something or other.

I remember one occasion in a scene with Diane Fletcher, who played Urquhart's wife – nothing particularly complicated – they were just sat together on a sofa watching some news item on TV. At the end of the item Diane merely had to lift the remote control and point it at the TV to turn it off. Well, I don't think she had used a remote before (or even seen anyone *else* use one). She just couldn't do it. Everything she did with it looked more and more unnatural and ridiculous. Ian was soon in a crying heap on the floor (as we all were) and I'm not sure to this day how we finished the scene.

The moment then took on a life of its own as other similar gestures later in the filming would remind them of it. Once, late at night, in a street scene with lots of expensive Extras who were about to go into overtime, Ian, as usual talking to camera, had to point his car-keys at his car to unlock the doors as he and Diane approached it. The combination of the end of a long tough day and the recognition of a hint of a ghost of similarity to the TV remote incident set them both off into shrieks of helpless laughter. The surrounding Extras were utterly bemused, which of course made the pair of them even more incapable.

Ian was *such* a pleasure to work with and some of the happiest days I've ever spent filming have been with him. He worked *so* hard and would not tolerate anyone working less hard than him, whether it might be a fellow actor or a member of the crew, but it was always *fun.*

Diane Fletcher – actress – Elizabeth Urquhart

Ian was a brilliant actor and a warm and humorous man of wit and charm. Working with him was one of the high points of my career. His skill, humour and hard work were an eye-opener to me. There was an enormous amount of pure learning of lines for Ian and not once did I observe him to be unprepared or falter in his faultless delivery. I tried to use him as a master class on technique, but we seemed to spend most of our scenes together giggling for no particular reason and having fun.

Susannah Harker – Mattie Storin

I remember reading the script for *House of Cards* and I hadn't read anything like it and was just blown away by it. It was a terrific script and part, and leapt off the page and I just wanted to do it.

What was strange was to play Ian's lover because I'd already played his daughter in *Troubles* [1988]. But as he was such a wonderful character and we were very much playing the truth of it, and the material was so strong, it was easy because we were totally inside the characters. We engaged professionally very well. But, I was just 25 and initially was very nervous because I couldn't think of him in that way at all and then I found a way.

He used to say things to me, as we changed gear into the passion of the relationship, like, "As you come towards me, just try dropping your voice a notch." And of course it worked wonderfully well because he was such a brilliant technician.

I was just astonished watching him in the studio in particular, when we did all his office stuff.

I recall watching a scene where Urquhart was taking a pee and he had to address the camera whilst obviously appearing to be having a pee and doing several other things, and it was just amazing.

It was a privilege to work with someone like Ian who was at the top of his game and had extraordinary concentration – you can just make it work. The other actor invites you to make it work and you know you can do it with them. He was simply a joy to work with from an acting point of view.

He used to be laughing with other people as I walked into the room – I was still young and very shy of course – he would tap under his chin whenever I was around as if to say, 'Keep your youth, you pretty little thing.'

He was funny and quite expressive and intense and I loved that. He would have the occasional explosion of temper, probably mostly out of frustration, but that was the way he worked and he needed to do that.

—•••—

Isla Blair – actress – Claire Carlsen, *The Final Cut*

When I did *The Waste Land* [a poem by T S Eliot] with Ian in the 1980's, for *Six Centuries of Verse* [Thames Television series, presented by Sir John Gielgud], I had a ghastly virus. I was standing off camera, due to give Ian my off-camera lines, when I was overwhelmed by this serious fit of coughing. I tried so hard *not* to cough that my eyes were streaming with the strain of not doing so, when finally Ian could see my predicament. Sweetly, he said, "Get Isla a glass of water. She is struggling to do the professional thing but she is choking here!" He wasn't impatient or cross, but utterly sympathetic and considerate.

When I did *The Final Cut*, on my first day I had an enormous dialogue scene with Ian – just him and me. It was all political stuff with an undercurrent of something else. The scene lasted about seven and a half minutes – the last really long scene on TV (it's all short bursts now – car chase, chat, car chase, etc.).

I was naturally nervous, despite having worked so hard on it on my own (no rehearsal now). The director called "Action!" and we were off. It was going okay, but I wasn't as good as I could have been. Ian 'dried'. Actually, I don't think for one minute that he did. It was his way of relaxing me – if he could dry it was all right if I did too. It was an act of professional kindness and I blessed him for it.

Nickolas Grace – Geoffrey Booza-Pitt, *The Final Cut*

Working on *The Final Cut* was just wonderful and we had some fantastic scenes together. I remember one scene where Ian has to say to me, "Geoffrey, have you a heart?"

Ian said to me that he was going to go a little further than what was in the script and put his hand inside my shirt. He put his hand in, felt around my chest, looked at me and said, "Do you think I am going too far?" and I said, "Never, Ian!"

8

From Brussels to the Falklands

The Gravy Train and *The Gravy Train Goes East*

Philip Hinchciffe – Producer

To know you have a leading actor who will drive a series, who is utterly dependable and yet who remains fresh and who surprises you with that extra touch of genius, is a rare luxury. Ian gifted that to us unfailingly.

The subject of the comedy dramas, *The Gravy Train* and *The Gravy Train Goes East*, penned by Malcolm Bradbury, was corruption and the power struggles within the European Economic Community and included the comic attempts by the British government, represented by the philandering, pompous Brussels official Michael Spearpoint, played by Ian, to win through against the other Member States. Spearpoint's battle-axe of a wife, Hilda, was played by Judi Parfitt, his mistress, Gianna, by Anita Zagaria and the unwitting 'hero' of the stories, Dorfmann, by Christopher Waltz.

James Cellan Jones – Director, *The Gravy Train Goes East*

When I was asked to direct *The Gravy Train Goes East*, I was very friendly with Malcolm Bradbury. I told Channel Four that Ian's role wasn't large enough, which Ian concurred with. We said that we wouldn't do it unless it was written up enormously, which was agreed and Malcolm was very happy to do.

It was extraordinary working again with Ian after so many years; it was as if *Eyeless in Gaza* had happened yesterday. We found ourselves sharing the same old jokes and the work became so easy that I would wake in the morning looking forward to the day with tremendous pleasure. Ian got on well with everybody and they were very happy memories.

Being with Ian and Maroussia once more was great and we had enormous fun. Whilst we were there, Ian won the BAFTA Award for Best Actor, for *House of Cards*. I said to him that we must all go out to dinner to celebrate. He responded, "I feel so shattered at having won this award, which was so undeserved, that I think I'd just like to stay in the hotel and rest." I asked Maroussia if she'd like to come and she said, "I certainly would!" and so we went out to celebrate Ian's award without him.

Philip Hinchcliffe – Producer

I worked with Ian on *The Gravy Train* for Channel 4. As soon as I received the first script from Malcolm Bradbury I knew that only one person should play Spearpoint – a bullying, self-centred bureaucrat, supremely confident of being in the right on all matters, with ludicrously blinkered tunnel vision – it was as if Malcolm had written the part especially for him. I was in Paris for early casting interviews with French and Italian actors and fortuitously, Ian was also there filming a series. I dropped the script off at his hotel and I think the same night I received it back with an excited note from him accepting the role. If only all casting was so easy!

Ian went on to give another *tour de force* performance in the first and a subsequent series, the first shot in Brussels and Austria, the second in Budapest. Again my abiding memory is of his energy, focus and undimmed enthusiasm on the set at all times.

There was always a lot of laughter on set during his scenes. It's not easy to make the crew laugh time and again; but it's even more difficult to balance perfectly on the tightrope of comedy drama, where the humour has to tiptoe alongside a plausible sense of reality and Ian was a past master at judging this in his performance.

I think he enjoyed his fame but to my mind he seemed a modest man. I suppose one could say he always placed the role above himself – it was the acting he loved – rather than stardom. His feet were firmly on the ground and I believe Maroussia was a great help to him by giving him the security and continuity in his life that enabled him to dive into each challenge with such gusto.

An Ungentlemanly Act

An Ungentlemanly Act tells the story of the Falklands invasion by Argentina in April 1982. It covers the period when the Governor of the Islands, Rex Hunt, is informed that Argentine forces are only hours away, the initial battle between the tiny force of Royal Marines on the island and the invasion force, and the Governor's surrender and expulsion from the island.

Rex Hunt was played by Ian, his wife, Mavis, by Rosemary Leach and their son, Tony, by a young Marc Warren. Bob Peck played the newly arrived commander of the forces on the island, Major Mike Norman, and Ian McNeice played the Chief Secretary, Dick Baker.

Being in the Falklands was a somewhat frustrating and, at times, lonely and boring experience for Ian:

> "I didn't have very much to do and Maroussia wasn't with me. On my first day off, I said I'd be all right because I liked walking. And so they all went off filming and I set off. Almost immediately I came to a barrier – 'No entry, mines' – and I turned and walked another way. After about 200 yards, I came to another barrier – 'No entry, mines'. So I had about three hundred yards in which to walk."

Stuart Urban – Director

Originally, Ian Holm was due to play Rex Hunt, but withdrew late on – when we were actually in the Falklands, preparing the film. We searched frantically for a replacement. Ian Richardson was very prompt in replying to our script. He read it and called us the same morning, saying that he would love to play the role. The film would otherwise very likely have been cancelled by the BBC.

Ian Richardson had been on our initial list, but we went with Ian H because not only was he more like Hunt in appearance, but his demeanour was more bureaucratic as opposed to Ian R's more patrician bearing.

We were so glad to get Ian Richardson when Ian Holm failed and he made it a big success by playing him more in the way that represented the perceived view of what the British colonial ruling class were like. In the end, I think it was all for the best because he changed the nature of the role and made it better. He was still true to the essence of the role and the man: a middle-ranking servant of the Empire who got his chance to strut upon the world stage and prove his mettle at the close of a hitherto rather undistinguished career.

Ian's most nervous moment was when Rex Hunt visited the set in the UK. We had taken every effort with the Hunts to consult with them, as had we by showing them the script. When we showed Hunt the film he was very moved by it, though retrospectively he appeared to change his mind. Perhaps it was to do with the depiction of his wife, Mavis, whose alcohol intake under the extreme pressure of a life-threatening situation was, in the opinion of most critics, not sensationalised or overdone. Furthermore, I believe Ian's portrayal could only have enhanced his reputation.

Ian worked fantastically well and was very technically dedicated and professional. We realised that he was very lonely on the Falklands without Maroussia and it must have been quite difficult for him.

Being on the island was like being transported back in time but we were also very conscious that we were in the middle of the South Atlantic, but in this little bit of Britain. And it was quite moving working at the places where the events at the outbreak of the war actually happened.

Ian could be very funny at times but he didn't suffer fools gladly. I remember one scene where an extra, playing a hydrographer, was meant to be destroying equipment to keep it from the Argentinians. This nervous young lad (whose first day on a film set this was) started smashing stuff up before I called "Action." Ian roared at him, "Boy, the word 'action' normally denotes the beginning of the action!" Of course, that had us all laughing.

In 2007, I did some speaking at public/academic events where the film was shown to mark the 25th Anniversary of the Falklands War. Ian's performance still drew so much attention and interest. It really was a privilege to have worked with him. He brought a lot to the drama and I believe only just missed out on winning the BAFTA for Best Actor. [Ian was also nominated for a Royal Television Society Award.]

Ian McNeice – Actor, Dick Baker

When I was at school, in Taunton, a trip to the RSC was organised and that was when I first became aware of Ian. We saw *All's Well* and *Coriolanus*, in which Ian had the lead role, and I can remember thinking he was extraordinary.

The first time I worked with him was on *Whoops Apocalypse* but we only had one scene together.

The next film we were both in was *The Year of the Comet*, which we filmed in Scotland. I lived in the States and Ian and Maroussia wanted me to get them some sleeping pills that were available there but not in the UK. Maroussia sent me a little note asking if I would come and see them. I knocked on the door of their hotel room, and when it was opened, saw that Maroussia was making supper for Ian on a hotplate and I thought, *how lovely*.

One of the cast, an American, was rather high-maintenance and far from punctual. Nothing was said till one day when everyone was just kept waiting too long. Ian let her know in no uncertain terms that her behaviour was unacceptable. It did the trick and she was never late again. He was a consummate artist and couldn't abide the lack of professionalism and courtesy not only to himself, but to all the cast and crew involved.

When we filmed *An Ungentlemanly Act*, because it wasn't possible for Maroussia to accompany Ian to the Falkland Islands, we had this man, completely lost without his absolute mainstay. I remember a few of us being flown over to Seal Island to see the seals and Ian talked incessantly, mostly about the RSC, all the way there, throughout the viewing of the seals and all the way back.

The only way we could get to and from the Falklands was on an RAF flight from Brize Norton. It was a troop-transporting plane and there were SAS rations, no hostesses and no booze. We were all glad to get back to the UK again, none more so than Ian, because it meant him being reunited with Maroussia.

In the early 1990's, Ian was involved in a number of other acting projects. Amongst his roles at that time, were a return to his Shakespearean roots as Polonius in the film of *Rosencrantz and Guildenstern are Dead*, written and directed by Tom Stoppard and starring Tim Roth, Gary Oldman, Iain Glen and Richard Dreyfus; a British diplomat in the adaptation of Barbara Taylor Bradford's *Remember*, with Claire Bloom playing his wife; a marvellously comic manager of the Paris Opera House in *Phantom of the Opera*, which starred Burt Lancaster and Charles Dance and was directed by Tony Richardson.

Foreign Affairs

In 1993, Ian made *Foreign Affairs*, a television movie, adapted from Alison Lurie's novel, starring Joanne Woodward as Vinnie Miner, a feisty American professor, and Brian Dennehy as Chuck Mumpson, an unsophisticated engineer who is her unwelcome travelling companion on a flight over from the States. She at first finds Chuck very irritating but he eventually gets under her skin and into her heart. Ian played Edwin, Vinnie's mischievous gay friend and confidante.

It was a happy time for Ian:

"Making *Foreign Affairs* was a lovely experience – one of my favourites. Joanne Woodward was such a simple, gentle person. I remember she said to me on the last day that her husband – the famous Paul Newman – had been planning to come that day and she'd wanted us to meet. She told me that she was so sorry that he was down with the 'flu and he'd be so cross not to have met me and I thought, so cross not to have met *me!*"

Joanne Woodward – actress

We had such a good time together and I just loved working with Ian.

I became enamoured of his performances as the prime minister in *House of Cards*. I still have that whole series just waiting to be watched all over again.

9

Return to the Theatre and Keeping Busy

For me and a great many other people, 1995 turned out to be a very special year. It marked Ian's first return to the stage since appearing in *Lolita* on Broadway in 1981.

I remember chatting to Andrew Davies whilst on a scriptwriting course in Devon a few months before Ian was due to appear in *The Miser*. Asking what Ian was like, Andrew told me that whenever he was in a room, you could sense his presence and were drawn to him like a magnet. Seeing him on stage for the first time, I realised that this magnetic force was also very much evident in his performances.

After several attempts, producer Duncan Weldon had managed to persuade Ian to return to his first love, the theatre – something he had always planned to do when the time and the project was right:

"For me, theatre will always provide a buzz, because that's where I began. It's where I belong and I walk onto the platform of any theatre, but particularly a Victorian theatre and you look out and there's all the gilt, ormolu, boxes and that sort of thing and you get a surge of such adrenaline and excitement which you cannot find anywhere else. And you certainly cannot find it walking into a studio, tripping over cables, with all the lights and cameras etc. You don't get the same buzz.

However, I have one great failing as a performer and it's that I have a very low toleration of boredom. If I'm doing the same thing for longer than six months maximum I just go bonkers.

When people come and try and tempt me back and I discover that it's for six months my heart sinks. That's because the people who come and pay to see you at the beginning of your six months are as entitled to the best that you can give as the people who come in the last week. To maintain that standard of professionalism is an enormous strain. I do change things because I get bored but the thing is to make it as worthwhile for the people at the end of the run as the beginning and that is a huge strain.

On the other hand, when you do something for the camera you can maybe do five, six, sometimes even ten takes of the same moment but, you know at the end of it that you have given the very best you can give and it's there for posterity. And you can forget it and go onto something else and that's the beauty of it.

Emotionally, though, my heart will always be there on a stage in a proscenium arch. It's magic – like very good sex."

The Miser

Ian's role in Ranjit Bolt's new adaptation of Moliere's *The Miser* was Harpagon, a consummate Scrooge. His son was played by Ben Miles and the matchmaker, Frosine, by Lesley Joseph. The production was directed by Nicholas Broadhurst.

It was an extremely energetic performance by Ian – too energetic as it turned out, as he ended up damaging his Achilles tendon early in the run and plans to transfer the play to the West End had to be abandoned.

Writing in *The Independent*, Paul Taylor said, "For several minutes, no intelligible word is spoken, as we follow Ian Richardson's sublimely funny miser through his early morning rituals in a mansion that's an Arctic temple of paranoid cost-cutting. Richardson, returning to the stage for the first time in 14 years after a distinguished career in television, gives a great performance and one that is frequently hilarious."

Echoing delight at his return to the boards, Robert Gore-Langton wrote in the *Daily Telegraph*, "His fishy glare and mesmeric voice are brought brilliantly to bear on Harpagon, the retentive French Scrooge. The part is a natural addition to Richardson's gallery of hypocrites and slimy schemers, and his performance is hilarious."

Maree Wilson – Admirer and Friend

To my great surprise and delight, the Chichester Festival Theatre announced that Ian would be appearing in *The Miser* for their 1995 season. I was so thrilled at the prospect of seeing Ian back where he belonged on stage after such a long gap and sent him a pair of cufflinks for good luck.

I remember travelling down to Chichester from London with friends. Reading an interview in the *Evening Standard*, it was mentioned that he had damaged his ankle. I was really worried in case he wouldn't appear. But even injured, he gave a very energetic performance.

The stage design for *The Miser* had a very Heath Robinson feel about it. The play, which was written in 1666, would be set in the present day and I had my doubts if this would work.

We first saw Ian as Harpagon, emerging from his bedroom in a hotel dressing gown, wearing a horrible red toupee and holding a chamber pot – what an entrance! He dominated the whole show from the word 'Go.' The play is really a satire on materialism and Harpagon was totally in love with money and the protection of his fortune. His house was full of security alarms. He lent money at an extortionate rate of interest even to his own son and wanted to marry the woman who is in love with the son. Finally, he was more distressed by the disappearance of his treasure chest than losing the young lady.

It was a wonderfully judged performance, very eloquent and full of brutal observation. It was a joy to see Ian back on stage, where he belonged.

I went round to the stage door afterwards and Ian and Maroussia were so charming. He thanked me for the cufflinks and showed me his badly swollen ankle.

I was to see him again in *The Magistrate* – another brilliant farcical performance – and several recitals, *The Hollow Crown* in Stratford in 2002, *The Echoing Green* with Judi Dench in 2003 and *Fond and Familiar* a week later in Winchester. In February 2004 I went to Toronto to see Ian in *The Hollow Crown* and was taken, along with friends, to lunch by Ian and Maroussia. I wonder how many other actors and performers gave so much time and showed so much appreciation to their fans and treated them as friends?

I next saw Ian in *Fond and Familiar* at Berkhamstead, this time with Judi and Geoffrey Palmer. Ian's performance that night had the audience gasping in admiration and wonder.

Cindy Lou Fiorina – Admirer and Friend

I was first captivated by Ian after seeing him as Nehru in *Mountbatten: The Last Viceroy*. I wrote to him and my first letter set off a 19-year correspondence.

After exchanging letters for seven years, I finally met him in 1995 at the Chichester Festival Theatre, where he was performing in *The Miser*. Unfortunately, I remember little about the show, apart from the fact that when Ian was on stage you were drawn to him like a magnet. What remains strongest in my memory is that first meeting backstage, when he came through the stairwell doors.

We continued writing so that when I met him once again in Stratford in 2002, when he was performing in *The Hollow Crown*, it was like seeing an old friend. There were some breathtaking moments during that show and Ian held the audience in the palm of his hand.

———

The Magistrate

Ian returned to Chichester in 1997, to play the well-meaning and increasingly befuddled Aeneas Posket in Pinero's *The Magistrate*. Fortunately there were no mishaps this time and, after a short tour the play ran at the Savoy Theatre in the West End for several months.

The play was again directed by Nicholas Broadhurst and the cast included Abigail McKern, Graham Crowden, Frank Middlemass and John Padden.

Writing in the *Daily Mail*, Michael Coveney described "Ian Richardson's gloriously self-important performance as the biter bit, the upright magistrate and practical philanthropist laid low…

Richardson's inimitable hauteur, strict profile and fierce delivery presents a statuesque grandee whose image is undermined with every new revelation."

Charles Spencer, in the *Daily Telegraph*, said, "Richardson beautifully captures the glassy-eyed desperation of the true farceur as, bewildered and battered, he clutches desperately at respectability while absent-mindedly sentencing his wife to seven days without the option. The great monologue describing the indignities that have befallen him is a real tour de farce."

—☙—

Abigail McKern – Actress – Agatha Posket

Working with Ian Richardson was, at first, a rather daunting experience. He came across as quite haughty and chilly and I felt like a schoolgirl who needed to keep on her toes, even though I was playing his wife. He was a total perfectionist and worked hard and fast, with no sufferance for laziness or for fools.

But I *loved* being on stage with him. His comic timing and technical brilliance and pace were a joy to behold and once he trusted you – you were in! I remember that the first time I made him laugh I was thrilled and felt huge relief.

He was a gentleman of the old school, with a twinkle in his eye and I greatly respected him.

—☙—

Ann Hopping – Admirer and Friend

I was so taken with Ian's performance in *House of Cards* – daring, witty and sometimes very funny – that I wrote to him. To my delight and surprise he answered and thereafter began an extensive correspondence.

At one point, when we were both in London, he invited me to lunch at the Garrick Club, where I met him and his lovely wife and 'partner in crime,' Maroussia. Ian was always a gentleman and generous to a fault. When he wasn't performing, he lived his life in the most unassuming way. More than a great actor, he was a great human being.

I was amazed by his performance in *The Magistrate* at the Savoy Theatre. He imbued the rather thankless role with a vigour contradicting his years – taking pratfalls like an athlete half his age.

Once on the boards he took over everything around him with the mastery of his craft. It was as if an invisible mantle floated over him, empowering him, illuminating him and the character so that they became one and the same.

That marvellous voice, the effortlessness of it all, still sends chills up and down my spine when I watch, for the umpteenth time, something like the extracts from *Richard II* – one of his most skilled performances – I was lucky enough to obtain.

What I remember most, however and will always treasure, is his sweetness bordering on shyness and the attention he paid to an unknown American whom he courteously and most graciously invited to lunch.

―――

Catherine The Great

Having served so well as a politician in the *House of Cards*, Ian again entered the world of politics to play Count Vorontzov in the miniseries, *Catherine the Great*, which starred Catherine Zeta-Jones in the title role, with Jeanne Moreau, Mel Ferrer and Omar Sharif amongst other cast members.

Reviewing the drama in *Variety Magazine*, Louise Nesselson commented, "Both servile and wise, Ian Richardson as one of Catherine's advisers is in a thesping class by himself, elevating every exchange to a much higher and always entertaining plane."

——◄••►——

Brian Blessed – Bestuzhev

Our relationship had a wonderful flowering when we came to film *Catherine the Great*.

We were waiting to film a scene and I told Ian how, many years ago at the National, Gielgud was in *Volpone* and I was in the *State of Revolution* playing Gorky. Gielgud had to pass me in the corridor every night and I would chase him and grab his arse and goose him. Well, Ian was begging me to stop telling him the story and during the takes he would fall apart with laughter. I could just quietly make the noise of Gielgud just before the takes and Ian would say, "I beg of you, Brian – please stop that – I just can't cope!"

At that time I never seemed to bother about looking after myself and getting myself coffee or anything. We were staying at this big, grand hotel and I was saying that I wished I had a coffee-maker and things like that. That evening, there was a knock on my door and there were Ian and Maroussia. They'd gone miles to a market and got this water heater, which was hard to find, and they brought me milk and sugar and coffee and tea and they just brought tears to my eyes. That was the kind of caring man he was and he was always checking if I had everything and the two of them just mothered me.

People assumed that he had a big ego, but in actual

fact he was such a self-effacing, unassuming, kind man. He had the most theatrical voice and there was the most wonderful style in all the things he did but he was basically an extremely normal human being.

He was a man of great stature and massive gravitas who wouldn't listen to fools, egotists or bullies. I place him right at the top with Gielgud, Richardson, Redgrave, Olivier and that sort of quality. There was a real mystery about his work and I think that was the source of his greatness.

It was lovely for me to play an entirely different type of part in *Catherine*. Our characters were political enemies at the beginning and by the end were the best of friends. By the end of filming, our relationship had been cemented too and it was a remarkable feeling. I think he is the only actor who has made my heart dance.

Paul McGann – Actor, Potemkin

One of the first things that I did was *Russian Night: 1941* – a Solzhenitsyn play on the BBC, round about 1983. It was the first time I met Ian and he was great in it. What was so memorable was that he made a kid feel so relaxed and welcome because it could have been quite nerve-wracking. But he was just charm itself and kept everyone laughing.

I loved him as an actor because he was such a great technician and everything he did seemed effortless. He was a good joker. Being young, I was trying so hard to please and impress and he punctured all that seriousness and took the piss, which I liked because it put me at ease. In *Russian Night* I was playing a young sergeant called Dygin and in between takes Ian started singing to the tune of *The Lambeth Walk*. He would sing, 'Doing the Dygin Walk' and mimicked both the way I walked and talked and nailed them.

It was great working again with Ian in *Catherine the Great*. My brothers, Mark and Stephen, were also in it and they really liked him because he was very kind to them. And he treated Catherine well. She was very young and carrying the thing and not everyone was an ally and some didn't respect her.

Most of it was filmed in Berlin and Ian and Maroussia were there and there was this big gang of us in this swanky hotel for weeks having the time of our lives.

I remember when we were waiting to do a scene in *Catherine* and we were standing in costume. Ian looked at me and told me that I looked like Napoleon – he'd just been reading a book on him. He said that if they were ever doing a film about Napoleon I should get my agent onto it.

We'd have a few sing songs and he'd often keep his counsel – he was very watchful and you never saw him go over the top but when he did chip in he became the life and soul of the party.

He wouldn't take any shit and he could fight his own corner – it was a large cast and there were some big personalities there. There were a few big egos and a few screaming matches and big sulks, but Ian was very calm and didn't get involved. He knew how to conduct himself – Marvin Chomsky, the director, thought he was just a class actor.

I remember Brian Blessed and Ian didn't want to pay the five-star room service prices and they would go over the street and then sneak across the foyer with some take-away sandwiches for their rooms.

Ian was a brilliant stage actor. He gave credence to the idea that there is nothing you can learn on a film set that can teach you much about how to walk out onto a big stage. Good stage actors can bring some of that learning onto a film set, but that doesn't work the other way around. Ian certainly had that and brought an ease, confidence and economy that translated to film.

The way he played to the camera in *House of Cards* wasn't an easy skill because you are trained to ignore the camera. He was brilliant at it – he had the stillness and reserve and twinkle that were so skilful and a great lesson to other actors. He came across as very self-assured and at ease with his talent and his skills.

When you were in a scene with him he was totally respectful. He hit the ball back to you and you got every opportunity from him to shine – it was a trade-off. That's the best accolade you could want as an actor.

The Treasure Seekers

In 1996, Ian played Haig, a bitter, reclusive Scottish moneylender, in a delightful adaptation of Edith Nesbit's classic novel about a motherless family of five who try to help out their inventor father, always with disastrous results. Amongst the cast were Gina McKee, Nicholas Farrell, Donald Sinden and Nigel Davenport.

John Sessions – Redman

I did *The Treasure Seekers* with Ian. I was playing the nice bank manager and he was playing the scurrilously wicked, miserly moneylender. The young lad Kris

Milnes, playing the eldest Bastable boy, was a bit nervous of working with the great Ian Richardson, who was of course delightful with him – patient and helpful.

I was always surprised that he never became a huge movie star. He should have been a Bond villain for a start, but instead he tended to be cast as the man from the Foreign Office. And he was such a fabulous actor. One of the greatest scenes in *Tinker Tailor Soldier Spy* was when he and Guinness were together at the end – he was just stunning.

———

Amongst other notable performances in a period filled with variety for Ian were the butler, Manley, in the Hollywood film, *BAPS*, which starred Halle Berry and Martin Landau; the title role in *The Canterville Ghost*; Mr Book, the shaven-headed leader of a sinister group of aliens in the film *Dark City*; Merlin in the TV movie, *A Knight in Camelot*, in which his character pitted his wits against an American scientist transported back to the Court of King Arthur, played by Whoopi Goldberg; Stephen Tyler in *The Magician's House* – a performance that had people making comparisons with William Hartnell's Doctor Who and suggesting that he should play the time-travelling doctor.

10

Dr Joseph Bell

1999 was an extremely busy year for Ian and a magical one for me. He performed his version of *The Seven Ages of Man* for a week to packed houses at the Yvonne Arnaud Theatre in Guildford. It presented a wonderful opportunity for someone like me, who had missed his 15 great years with the Royal Shakespeare Company in the 1960's and 1970's. To see and hear him perform a range of roles from Shakespeare's plays was a joyful experience and gave me a flavour of what it must have been like sitting in the audience in Stratford or at the Aldwych in London.

I was staying in London with Shirley Jacobs, who has a website devoted to Ian's career. After the performance, he invited Shirley and me to go for a drink. When we left the pub, Ian insisted that he and Maroussia walk us part of the way back to the train station. We exchanged hugs and went our separate ways but when we'd got about 100 yards further down the road this voice came booming out towards us, "It's just down there!" I remember laughing, because Ian was wearing a cap to give him anonymity and yet as soon as he opened his mouth, that glorious voice was unmistakeable.

He generally wore hats and often a large pair of glasses to disguise his appearance when out and about, but of course the camouflage was always redundant the second he spoke.

I saw Ian a further three times that year – and all in my

hometown, Glasgow. In July he received an Honorary Doctorate of Drama from the Royal Scottish Academy of Music and Drama where he had studied and was a Fellow.

Murder Rooms: The Dark Beginnings of Sherlock Holmes

A couple of months after receiving his doctorate, Ian returned to Glasgow to star as Dr Joseph Bell, who had been Arthur Conan Doyle's professor at Medical School and was thought to be his inspiration for Sherlock Holmes, in *Murder Rooms: The Dark Beginnings of Sherlock Holmes*. As a 'wannabe' scriptwriter, I'd asked the production company if I could observe some exterior filming.

I watched a scene being filmed, principally involving Robin Laing, who was playing Doyle. Afterwards, I met up with Ian and Maroussia and Ian invited me to join them for a meal in his trailer. I remember Aly Bain, the renowned Scottish fiddler, who had a small role in the drama and had been in the scene I'd observed, popping his head round the door to say goodbye.

He had received an Honorary Doctorate at the same time as Ian and it got us talking about the ceremony. Ian told me that he had had his photo taken with all the Drama graduates. I said that the students must have been honoured and Ian's immediate response was, 'No, I was honoured to have my photo taken with them.'

Whilst there, Ian decided that I should watch filming that would be far more beneficial than the scene I'd observed. He disappeared out of the caravan and returned a while later to announce that he'd got permission from various people for me to be allowed to witness one of the main scenes being filmed.

A couple of weeks later, I spent a magical day in Glasgow's Pollok House watching a major scene – mirroring the one in *The Sign of Four* in which Holmes examines a pocket watch given to him by Watson and makes deductions from it – being rehearsed and filmed and another one being rehearsed.

I was able to witness at first hand Ian's utter professionalism, dedication and attention to the minutest detail. But more, I saw how at ease and friendly he was with all the cast and crew, treating everyone with courtesy and as equals and joining in with practical jokes and keeping everyone laughing.

Filming the drama, scripted by David Pirie, proved to be a happy return for Ian to the city he had studied in:

"A most moving moment for me was filming Joseph Bell, because Bell was a lecturer in medical studies at Edinburgh University. However, at the time they chose to shoot the film, the Edinburgh Festival was on and there was no way we could get a film unit into Edinburgh University. So, we all moved up the Byres Road and into Glasgow University.

We started there on my first morning, lecturing to a group of students. Not only was I lecturing in an old lecture hall where I myself had sat as a student, but as I opened my mouth to speak, the famous clock struck ten, which was the noise it made when we picked up our pens and began our examinations. It was, for a very emotional, fey Scotsman, an extraordinary experience. I loved it and I remembered, with Joe Brady and Annie Byers and Anne Kirsten, finishing our lectures and going into the McEwans pub in the Byres Road. And all we could afford was a half pint. All sorts of memories came back.

I owe an enormous debt to Glasgow, to the Drama School in particular, but more in a kind of inspirational way to the University, because it was there that I was informed by one of my lecturers [Shakespearean scholar, Professor Peter Alexander] that actually I possibly had a career in classical theatre. And I would never have thought of it had that seed not been planted there in Glasgow University. So Glasgow for me is a place I regard with huge gratitude and affection."

The story told of how Arthur Conan Doyle, whilst studying

medicine at Edinburgh University, became clerk to Dr Joseph Bell. Bell had already been assisting the police in murder investigations and Doyle soon became involved in the process.

The relationship between Bell and Doyle is almost one of a father and son, Bell having lost his only son to peritonitis and Doyle's father being a drunkard and unstable. Dundee-born actor Robin Laing and Ian established a strong rapport.

Like the character he played, Ian was a generous and inspiring mentor to Robin, who described him as a 'lovely, lovely man' and acknowledged that he was extremely supportive and helpful.

In an interview with David Wroe in *The Age*, on 25 May, 2000, Robin Laing said, "You'd feel this tugging and he'd just be looking at you, not saying anything, just looking at you sideways and pulling you slightly towards him. You'd say, 'What you doin'?' and he'd say, 'Feel that? There's more light on your face, you look better like that.'"

For Ian, playing Joseph Bell was a joy – and someone much more akin to him in nature than Francis Urquhart:

"Joe Bell was my friend and I loved living his life. I would like to think that I'm as generous and as kind-hearted as Joseph Bell was.

With Francis Urquhart, which was a complete characterisation, I steeped myself in his persona. With Joseph Bell it wasn't necessary to do that except to say that I taught myself certain aspects of medical surgery lingo. I needed to know aspects of people's bodies to be looking for and to know in simplest terms how to take someone's pulse, what was here in the pulse region of the neck, how to feel around the stomach area for any possible indications of a malignant tumour. I needed to know all that, but that was easy.

I did an enormous amount of research into him. He actually had a rather high-pitched voice and was very much your Morningside speaker. And I thought if I'm going to make this man a hero, no, I couldn't make him speak with a high-pitched Morningside accent, so I lowered my tones.

When I went out with *The Hollow Crown* to Australia I visited the island of Tasmania. I was playing in the main theatre in Hobart and this lady visited me and said that she was the great great-niece of Joseph Bell. She had all this wonderful information about his background and all the rest of it. We kept in touch and I sent her all my Joseph Bell recordings on DVD. I received letters from her in which she said that 'it's impossible for all of us not to consider you to be a member of our family.'"

Following the success of the initial drama, a series of four more stories was commissioned, with Charles Edwards replacing Robin Laing as Doyle. The four dramas were *The Patient's Eyes*, *The Photographer's Chair*, *The Kingdom of the Bones* and *The White Knight's Stratagem*. Simon Chandler appeared in the first three as Inspector Warner and amongst other performers were David Hayman, Anton Lesser, Ronald Pickup, Ian McNeice and Rik Mayall.

Murder Rooms was very well received and Ian won a Sherlock Award for his portrayal of Bell.

Paul Seed – Director, *The Dark Beginnings of Sherlock Holmes*

I worked with Ian several more times after the Urquhart pieces, not least on *Murder Rooms: The Dark Beginnings of Sherlock Holmes*. Joseph Bell was in many ways, I think, the closest Ian ever came to playing himself on screen. They shared that utter dedication to finding the truth and logic behind a problem and then relishing the solving of that problem – and *always* with wit, warmth and humour.

Paul Marcus – Director, *The Photographer's Chair* and *The White Knight's Stratagem*

I loved working with Ian and getting into intense dialogues with him about scenes. He was beyond professionalism in his attitude and had a tremendous lack of self-importance and pomposity. He was greatly appreciative of the level of craft that people brought to bear on a production.

Dr Joseph Bell was a role that Ian felt very strongly about because he identified greatly with the character. He wanted it to be the third part of his creative screen legacy along with Bill Haydon and Francis Urquhart.

Murder Rooms got the most wonderful responses from the media and the public and our co-production partners were begging the BBC to do another series. But for what could only have been political reasons the BBC decided not to go ahead with it and Ian felt very let down.

There were three things that I loved about Ian in the role. Firstly, he was such a forensic user of language – so clear and precise and that paralleled with the nature of Bell's mind. Ian relished the opportunity to express Bell's thoughts.

Secondly, the kind of energy of Bell who, like many eminent Victorians, led several lives all wrapped into one. He helped the police solve murders and was the forerunner of the science of forensics, wrote articles about the Scottish countryside and was a church elder. Ian admired him greatly. I loved the richness of his range of activities and the energy about him. He had so much vigour in his performance.

Thirdly, the humour. Bell had a mischievous twinkle and sense of irony. In the whole conduct of the quasi father/son relationship between Bell and Doyle, Ian brought so much humanity and humour into it.

It would have been absolutely impossible for anyone else to have played that role so well. Ian set to work as many weeks beforehand as he could to prepare himself and brought extensive knowledge with him. At the same time, he had great flexibility and was open to suggestions. He expected though, quite rightly, that a director shared his depth of research – and enjoyment – I think that's why we got on so well. And he liked the idea that I shared a similar classical theatre background.

In *Murder Rooms* he had rare lapses when his recollection of dialogue let him down and it would cause hysterics. In *The Photographer's Chair*, in one scene he arrived in the mortuary, strode over to a corpse and lifted a hand. He should have said, "I doubt if there's another man in Portsmouth of this stature, wealth and digital deficiency." Instead Ian declared, "Ah, the most digital fingers in Portsmouth."

In *The White Knight's Stratagem*, Ian was meant to be reeling off a list of names – it was of famous people who were ambidextrous – Michelangelo, Leonardo Da Vinci, Benjamin Franklin and Sir Edwin Landseer. He managed the list effortlessly each time, but as we moved the camera around the room he recited the list perfectly until he came to the end when he said 'Sir Edwin Landfill'. I was laughing so much I couldn't say 'cut' and Rik Mayall and Charlie Edwards had gone too. Ian was baffled. "But the camera wasn't on me – you could have carried on." He was oblivious to the hysteria he had created.

The only time I saw him lose his temper was when we were filming a scene using a pyrotechnic effect. We knew that the space would fill up with a great deal of smoke. The First Aider was very nervous because there were onlookers nearby and referred to them as 'rubber-neckers'. Of course Maroussia was one of the onlookers and Ian went up the wall at the perceived insult to his beloved wife and to the others, which was rather magnificent.

I worked with Ian again in 2003 on *Imperium: Nero*, which was filmed in Tunisia. He played an elderly senator and gave a marvellous performance, which I likened to that of Edward Heath in his old age. He used all of his experience and qualities of irony. He gave the part such depth and range. Ian was happy to be working again with the writer Paul Billing, whose scripts were clear, economical and specific.

John Simm played Caligula and Ian knew of him as a working class contemporary actor and was so admiring of his received pronunciation and the intelligence he brought to his role. He was very capable of enjoying the work of other actors.

Meg Speirs – Makeup Designer

I just adored Ian. He was such a delightful person and we got on and worked extremely well together. We always used to have great laughs and I absolutely loved working with him.

He was so natural and got on with everyone. He was never rude and rarely impatient – except with himself – but so forgiving of others.

I remember when we were filming the first *Murder Rooms* in Pollok in Glasgow, we always had a laugh about Ian's regal tone. One day I was fixing his wig and Maroussia came in and presented him with a tea cosy with a royal crown on it, she'd just bought in the shop in Pollok House. She popped it on his head and we were all hysterical.

He was a very gentle, beautiful, thoughtful man. And when we were filming in Glasgow he loved being back in the place where he'd studied – and the honesty of the people.

The four-part series was mainly shot in various locations in England. However, when we were filming the last episode we went up to Edinburgh for a couple of weeks and Ian and Charlie Edwards were doing a scene where they were being driven along a cobbled street in an open carriage. The horse kept farting all the time and they used to come out of the carriage green from the fumes and Ian was in hysterics. He and Charlie used to corpse all the time.

Joseph Bell was a wonderful part for him – he just was Bell and absolutely slipped into his skin.

One day he was filming a very long and difficult speech in a university lecture theatre and kept apologising when he couldn't get it just right. When he did finish the speech he got a huge round of applause and everybody stood up and cheered him.

—◆◆◆—

Stephen Gallagher – Writer, *The Kingdom of the Bones*

Ian was an actor of astonishing power and magisterial presence on stage and screen; away from it a humble, engaging and truly likeable person. For any writer, it was an honour just to hear him speak one's words.

My first meeting with him was at the Bloomsbury

Central Baptist Church in March, 2001. It's an imposing building in the middle of a block close to the Shaftesbury Theatre. BBC Films had taken upstairs rooms for the table read of my *Murder Rooms* episode, *The Kingdom of the Bones.* I thought it was an exceptional series idea in classic BBC style and I was happy to be on board. The concept was a blend of fact, fiction and metafiction – Bell wasn't Sherlock Holmes but had provided Doyle with some elements for his fictional creation and now here was the fictional Bell, playing a Holmesian role.

I always look forward to read-throughs. There are few happier sights than an actor with a job and at a read-through you get a room full of them. And if you're really lucky there's cake. This time around, though, I was slightly nervous. Ian Richardson was playing the role of Joseph Bell and was a big name in anybody's book – an old school, highly regarded, professional who would, I can imagine, have been equally at home on a bill with Henry Irving or Beerbohm Tree as on a modern film set.

I'd first been impressed by the offhanded authority of his Bill Haydon in Arthur Hopcraft's adaptation of *Tinker Tailor Soldier Spy;* the air of dignity and acceptance with which he dabbed blood from his nose after a rough interrogation treatment struck me as an acting master class all in itself.

I felt a bit excited and a bit intimidated. I needn't have worried. He arrived without ceremony and demanded no special attention. The most magnetic actor on the screen was the most diffident man in the room. During a break I went over and introduced myself. I think I just babbled a bit. I introduced my daughter, who had a small part as a circus girl with a line and a song. Ian's son Miles, who was busy with RSC duties and hadn't been able to make the read-through, would be opening our film as the explorer Everard Im Thurn.

I mentioned a short documentary I'd recently seen on BBC3 [*One Foot in the Past*], in which Ian took a walk up Arthur's Seat in Edinburgh and reminisced about his youth in the city. "Oh that thing'" he said. "I've no idea why, but they do keep showing it."

The next time we met was on location at the old American University in Bushey, a complex of redbrick buildings that's been used in movies from *Lucky Jim* to *Harry Potter*. The frontage was our Southsea museum, the yards around the back housed our wintering circus troupe and inside the dining hall, the art department had erected a fairground marquee for interior cover. This time Ian was mostly in character and in costume and cut a genuinely commanding figure. He'd played Sherlock Holmes on screen, but his Joseph Bell was a distinctly different creation: sharp and intelligent, but with a warmth unique to the character.

As we talked between set-ups, I realised that his research for the part went way beyond the page. He lent me a book on Bell, which I read and returned, and some photocopies of his research that I was to keep for future reference. None of us doubted that this was a series of continuing potential.

The film, directed with grace and precision by Simon Langton and with a marvellous turn by John Sessions as Bell's colleague, William Rutherford, gave me more of a sense of satisfaction than almost anything else in my CV. The series as a whole was a success with both the critics and the audience.

So naturally, it was cancelled. A second series was planned and there was funding in place from the States, but the plug was pulled by the BBC before they were commissioned.

But at least I got to work with Ian Richardson.

David Stuart Davies – provides extracts from an interview with Ian

I spent an enchanting day down at Bray Studios watching the filming of an episode from the *Murder Rooms* series and interviewing Ian again and he was more than happy to talk about his role as Bell and the new series. Our conversation revealed quite clearly the dedication and study Ian gave to this part, as he did to all his others:

"*Murder Rooms* took me completely by surprise when it came along the first time. And quite frankly I didn't think that much would come of it. But it's been enormous fun. And I'm delighted to say that thanks to purists like Charles [Edwards] and myself they've stuck fairly honestly to the format which conforms with the reputation and memory of Bell and similarly of Conan Doyle himself."

There were several literary influences on Doyle – the works of Poe and Gaboriau for instance, but Bell was the only living influence:

"You must know the story about Robert Louis Stevenson. He was out in Samoa and Doyle sent him a copy of his first Holmes novel and Stevenson read it and wrote back congratulating him and said, 'But surely this is my old friend Joe Bell!' He actually recognised Bell from the story."

[While Ian was in the middle of speaking to David, one of the technicians working on the film came forward and interrupted him to say how much he had enjoyed his performance in *House of Cards*. Ian broke off in mid-sentence to thank the man kindly for his wishes and then without so much as a beat picked the sentence up and continued with it as though there had been no interruption at all.]

In your case we have a complicated situation where Doyle, to a large extent, is basing Sherlock Holmes on Bell, you've played Sherlock Holmes and now you're playing Bell. How close...:

"Well, they are very close in terms of technique, but not in their personalities. Whereas Sherlock Holmes is single minded and capable, on occasion, of unintentional cruelty, Bell was never capable of that kind of harshness. The homework I did twenty-odd years ago in order to play Sherlock Holmes shortened my journey of exploration this time quite substantially.

I debated long and hard when I was asked in one scene, for instance, to enjoy a whisky and soda. I decided that despite Bell's deeply religious background that as a Scotsman he would see no particular harm in that so I was able to meet Sherlock Holmes in that sense because they always seemed to have a flask of something with them. That may seem rather trite but it is only by attending to those tiny things that you build up the composite whole."

And Bell is a warmer, more rounded individual:

"I think so. You see, Bell was a man whose first and foremost object in life was the saving of life.

There was an incident in his young days when he was on his rounds and came across a child who was in an advanced state of diphtheria. He had not the wherewithal to save the child's life. He couldn't perform an instant tracheotomy, so he put a tube down the child's throat, which was filling up, and choking it to death, and sucked the poison out.

Unfortunately for Bell, he actually swallowed some of it and he was ill for a long time and that's why he walked with a kind of a limp thereafter. I don't walk with a limp in the series because it would look peculiar but I use a walking stick a lot of the time for the same reason."

It sounds as though you could give the writers a master class on the character:

"I could. They only have to ask."

Have you been involved in changing certain aspects of his character and behaviour?:

"Yes, quite serious things where I have been asked to do something that Bell would never do. I won't give you instances because it would immediately identify which film, which director and which writer! But I will say that people like David Pirie are very modest when it comes to suggestions for a little textual alteration.

For example, in David's very first *Murder Rooms*, I had to repeat the diagnostic evidence I gleaned from Doyle's watch, just as Sherlock Holmes does with Watson's in *The Sign of Four*. In those days the Latin plural for data would be, 'there aren't any data.' David had written in his script, 'there isn't any data.' In the twenty-first century that is perfectly acceptable. Not acceptable in Bell's and Holmes' day. So I put that right and David went out with his mobile phone and rang someone up to check and said, 'Yes, you're quite right.'"

I cherish my very brief times with him. As well as a great actor, he was a warm man, enthusiastic about his craft and dedicated to it. Ian Richardson holds a unique place in Sherlockian film history as being the only actor to play both Holmes and the inspiration for the character, Joseph Bell. And he did so brilliantly.

11

The Owl and The Crown

Gormenghast

"Perching on a mantelpiece flapping my elbows for a whole day made me feel a bit stiff on the morrow."

In 1999, Ian played Lord Groan, in the BBC adaptation of Mervyn Peake's great opus, *Gormenghast*. In portraying the descent into madness of the already fragile Earl, weighted down by the rituals of Gormenghast and a harridan of a wife, he gave a heart-rending, memorable performance.

When Ian got the part, he commented:

"It's a lovely role. My character goes mad, thinks he's an owl and sits on the mantelpiece going 'Hoo!' It should be fun."

He obtained tapes of owls to study before filming began and special contact lenses to give him more of an owl-like appearance. Physically, impersonating a bird was a little challenging.

According to Peter Paterson, writing in the *Daily Mail* on the 18 January, 2000, the Earl was "played to perfection". Although the production was well received by lovers of the book, the critics were divided on its success.

Commenting in *The Times* on the 25 January, Joe Joseph said, "Lord knows we're looking for reasons to praise *Gormenghast*. Last night we had that reason in Ian Richardson's mesmerising descent into madness. The rest of the cast looked on in horror as Richardson's Lord Groan took it into his head that he was an owl. Or maybe the panic was because they sensed that Richardson's imminent disappearance would rob the series of its biggest draw."

Producer Estelle Daniel, in her diary entry of 28 May, reproduced in *The Art of Gormenghast: The Making of a Television Fantasy*, (HarperCollins Entertainment; BBC TV tie-in edition, January 2000) said, "The King Lear scene. Groan and Fuchsia outside the burnt-out library pretending the fir cones are books. The last weeks have been marked by an anticipation of this scene. A full blooded and intensely moving performance from Ian Richardson."

After describing the scene, which she called, "beautiful and passionate," she continues to talk about what happens when nine of Mervyn Peake's grandchildren visit.

"They come on set to watch Ian in the big scene. I worry about the distraction, still want them to see it. But Ian comes round between takes and entertains them with largesse. He seems in the greatest and richest of humours. The performance is assured – echoes of many of the Shakespearian characters he inhabits are combined and the ground feels very solid."

Celia Imrie – Lady Groan

Ian was a glittering icon I grew up with and I couldn't believe my luck when I got the chance to work with him. The first time was in 1997, in the *Pleasure and Repentance* recital programme in The Swan at Stratford, in memory of Brenda Bruce. Up until then Ian was someone I admired from afar and I was quite flummoxed by the whole idea of being on stage with him, even though our moment together was only brief.

Working with such a revered Shakespearian performer

was thrilling, though he never played the grand veteran older actor at all. Sometimes, though not always, generations can be rather divided, and the older ones stick together and complain about the younger ones, and vice versa but there was none of that with Ian ever.

When we played the bizarre Lord and Lady Groan in *Gormenghast*, I loved, when I heard that Ian, in order to play the owl-like Lord, had got the BBC Wildlife information tapes on birds to observe their mannerisms. I can remember him jumping up on to our table during a banqueting scene and turning himself absolutely into an owl and flying down before our very eyes. It was just wonderful.

I had to act most of my scenes with this extraordinary albino crow on my shoulder and I knew from that strange experience, how remarkably accurate Ian's movements were. At the same time as being extraordinary, he made his bird-like behaviour completely normal, as though it was the most natural thing in the world.

In *Gormenghast* he had a marvellous crown and cloak. He wore his costumes like a French actor – as if he wore them every day – but he had a particular aura of whatever period he was in. He was out of the ordinary, though completely natural.

When we filmed *The Canterville Ghost*, I remember thinking how brilliant he was at being a ghost, because he was playing him very mischievously.

In that respect it made him much more interesting, instead of making spooky noises around the house as you might expect a phantom to do. He was very down to earth and charming, with such a twinkle in his eye. He was a very witty actor and didn't take himself too seriously, while being utterly committed – he never appeared to be acting. He just made things look so easy and yet he was very physical and threw himself into everything he had to do.

Ian and Dame Judi had a huge affection and admiration for one another, and when we were filming *The Canterville Ghost* I asked if he'd mind having a Polaroid photograph taken of the two of us together to send Judi for fun, to make her green – showing her what fun I was having during the great treat of working with him too.

The thing I loved most about him before I met and worked with him, was the naughty glint he had in his eye, which you saw when he was acting and which was magnified and put to such brilliant use when he played Urquhart. Playing to the camera had never been done quite like that before and I thought that it took some nerve. He really flirted with his viewing audience.

He made an interesting transition, because the RSC acting of his youth was very different from what we now witnessed, and yet he managed to straddle both. Urquhart was an absolute one-off – I don't believe that anyone has managed to touch that performance and I can't think of another person in the country who could have commanded the role so superbly.

Also, I should imagine that he had to do monologues about five pages long and I don't think I ever saw him with a script in his hand when we worked together. He was one of these people who knew everything, yet looked as if he was making it up on the spot in a way that was just mesmerizing to watch.

There's no question that he should have been knighted. And there really isn't anyone else you could say he was like – he was absolutely unique.

John Sessions – Prunesquallor

I was so excited playing Prunesquallor in *Gormenghast* – it was my favourite role. Ian all too clearly was your absolutely proper actor – the one who had done the serious stuff. I remember watching him sitting up on the mantelpiece when his character thought he was an owl. I think he quite liked that because there was a rather barmy side to him.

Ian had that Jesuitical severity about him. He was never fashionable, with turned-up collars or being hip. But he possessed this astonishing vocal instrument that could be like a viper gliding through velvet at times, with those wonderful little undertones that could be very, very smooth or a little bit airy and it was so governed and toned and honed by all that thrust. And when Helen Mirren, Derek Jacobi and Richard Pasco read at his Memorial Service I'd like to think that Ian was looking down from somewhere and saying, 'Yes, that's the way to do it.'

Ian was much more of the Gielgud tradition, which was a French one, than the Olivier one. He knew he didn't have to sing the verse but that it had a dynamic range to it and that's how it worked.

Then there was the barmy side. There was a great little scene in *Blunt: The Fourth Man*, which he made with Anthony Hopkins. Ian, as Blunt, was sitting on a bus and there was a little specky kid with a cap staring at him and Ian suddenly pulled this gargoyle face and it reminded me of an almost wackiness to him. Most people are only aware of this rather severe, suave, punctilious figure but he could pull some Scottishness on you as well.

The only thing that really bothered him was

incompetence. And he expected to be treated with respect – not like the Queen of Sheba – but for others to have some awareness of what he had done, because such a large body of his work was with the RSC.

———

The Hollow Crown

In April 2002, Ian went on the tour of Australia and New Zealand with Donald Sinden, Derek Jacobi, Diana Rigg and musician Stephen Gray, performing John Barton's RSC production of *The Hollow Crown*.

The tour was highly successful, playing to sell-out audiences and garnering high praise. Writing from Perth, Ian commented:

> "New Zealand is behind us, still extolling our triumph: and I must confess that our reception and success has far exceeded my expectations. We are all in good form and enjoying each other's companionship – a rare and precious thing."

The production then played to packed audiences at the Royal Shakespeare Theatre in Stratford for the week in July that year, with Janet Suzman in place of Diana Rigg, and again in Australia and New Zealand the following year.

At the Princess of Wales Theatre, Toronto, in January, 2004 Ian and Donald were joined by Vanessa Redgrave and Alan Howard for a five-week run of *The Crown*.

———

Sir Donald Sinden

I first did *The Hollow Crown* in 1964 – with Peggy Ashcroft. In 2002, with Diana Rigg, Derek Jacobi, Ian and myself, we took *The Crown* around Australia and New Zealand. It was a lovely experience. Off and on stage we all got on wonderfully well together. You have to have a happy group when you are such a small Company and we certainly were. Ian and Maroussia were an absolute joy to be with.

I was very envious of Ian having Maroussia with him. Later, in Toronto, we all stayed in hotels except for them. They booked apartments whenever possible when they were away working and I remember that after the performances Ian and Maroussia would head back to their apartment and she would cook for them.

Going to Australia and New Zealand – especially the first time in 2002 – was very exciting. We got a terrific reception and they seemed delighted to see us. Wellington, in New Zealand, was a slight shock. We met the local impresario and we were told we were opening at the Fowler Centre, which seated 2,300 people! And it was absolutely packed out.

In Auckland, we played at a converted cinema with a 2,900 capacity. It was built in the '30's and the auditorium had been decorated in dark blue, with Eastern scenes and camels and lions on the walls. At every performance, a quarter of an hour before the start, the lights go out and the audience can look up to the ceiling and see the stars of the Southern Hemisphere come out and move across until the dawn. When the curtain goes up it's an anticlimax and, to make matters worse, on either side of the proscenium arch sat two golden lions with green eyes that flashed throughout the performance.

It was in Adelaide, I think, that we did a schools matinee. We were in the wings waiting to come on and the noise from the young people was unbelievable. We wondered what to do and after some hesitation marched onto the stage and bowed to the audience. The noise got louder. We asked for the house lights to be put up and the noise got worse. Ian eventually stood up and began, 'For God's sake let us sit upon the ground,' and they started to cheer while he continued the speech. We did the whole performance through the noise.

Early on the tour, I told Ian a story from the time when I was in Japan with the RSC. He thought it was the funniest thing he had heard and whenever we were in company he asked me to repeat it. I must have told it about 10 times. I repeated it at his Memorial Service. Ian could be wonderfully outspoken at press conferences and he was always very voluble. If he didn't like something he would always speak his mind, forcibly. The rest of us happily sat back and let him have a good gripe.

Each time Ian opened *The Hollow Crown* with the *Richard II* speech he did it absolutely beautifully and he did a frightfully good, haughty Charles I. As a stage actor, his verse speaking was simply wonderful. I've never known anyone who could speak so quickly – he was like a machine gun – and yet as clearly as he did.

—◆◆◆—

Janet Suzman – Actress

On a tour, somebody's birthday is quite sure to crop up along the way to provide the perfect excuse for a party. So it was with us in Hobart when Ian's birthday duly came rolling along and, luckily, not on a matinee day. So, we convened a cast-and-crew surprise lunch in a lovely fish restaurant with lots of great New Zealand white wines and delicious south Atlantic fish.

An endless series of risqué stories went the rounds, fond speeches were made and altogether a great fuss was made of Ian, which made him very happy, I think. The affection of one's peers and colleagues is always very inspiriting and lots of laughter is the best birthday treat of all.

I don't suppose he often had occasion to use the rather elegant silver hip-flask I gave him, but it so suited his masterly demeanour. He bore, I always thought, the lofty air of someone far too grand to stoop to a mere glass in the midst of a thirsty adventure in the Antipodes.

—••—

Lorraine Bonecki – Admirer and Friend

It all began when I sent Ian Richardson a story I had written for him. I never expected more than a thank you and an autograph, but this was actually the start of a wonderful nine-year correspondence. I was deeply honoured by his encouragement and praise.

His letters were lovely little literary gems filled with wit and charm. He was not above a pun or a humorous remark – usually laced with a dash of gentle sarcasm. He would sometimes mention his career, but he most often touched on little everyday things – solving crosswords, bottling damson wine, taking a walk on his Devon estate – and always, always he spoke of his great love for his family.

I had an opportunity to meet Ian and his wife, Maroussia, when he performed in *The Hollow Crown* in Toronto in January of 2004. The trip itself was a disaster for me. I had a terrible cold, and I endured an almost fourteen-hour train ride from Chicago. The way back was even worse. I was up at 4 am to catch a train that never came and ended up on a crowded bus all the way home. Despite all this, I would have done it again in an instant for a chance to see Ian Richardson on stage.

As much as I've always admired Ian's on-screen performances, there was something absolutely magical when he appeared in the theatre. He certainly held me spellbound throughout *The Hollow Crown* with his rich, mellifluous voice, his subtle nuances of character, and his great animation of spirits. I particularly recall Ian's portrayal of a sombre, defiant Charles I at the trial for his execution, followed by a lightning shift to a foppish, addle-brained Charles II, who could hardly remember the name of his future bride.

After the show, the Richardsons invited me out to dinner, together with a member of the stage management team. It was the most thrilling night of my life. Ian greeted me with a gallant kiss on the hand and he was, as always, the epitome of courtesy and kindness. He teased me about my long train ride and kept us all amused with his marvellous theatrical anecdotes. I recall ordering dessert simply because I didn't want the evening to end.

Ian Richardson was indeed an actor of tremendous depth and power, but I shall always remember him most as a kind and caring individual who was never too busy to dash off a cheery line or two to a friend.

—◆◆◆—

Anne Gilhuly – Admirer and Friend

In 1997, I realized that every actor who'd ever impressed me on screen had cut his teeth on theatre, often with the Royal Shakespeare Company. So when one of the local papers praised a BBC production starring some RSC actor I'd never heard of, I taped it.

I watched *House of Cards* in one sitting and *To Play the King* the next night and Ian Richardson dazzled me.

In 2002, when I learned he'd soon be at Stratford in *The Hollow Crown*, I decided to make the trip over from New York. Sharon Mail said she'd try to arrange an introduction.

The Hollow Crown was a terrific showcase for four brilliant actors and Ian was all that I'd hoped he'd be. His Bradshaw, sentencing Charles I to death, made me think of sharks circling a tiny boat – at one point I literally shivered. Moments later, as Charles II describing his wedding night with the aid of a fluffy feather, he had me laughing so hard I could hardly breathe.

After the show, Sharon, Shirley Jacobs and I crowded into the dressing room with Ian and Maroussia. What a sweet, gracious, friendly, funny, unpretentious, utterly charming person he turned out to be. He enthused about his cast mates – he'd never worked with Sir Derek before and adored him – and fumed about a loud, persistent cougher in the audience whom I hadn't even noticed. Sharon said that the look Ian gave the cougher, 'would have curdled milk' and Ian admitted, "I got a bit of a bollocking – pardon my French – from Janet at the interval."

It was great fun the next day to watch Ian hold court at the stage door. Someone handed him a photo of himself as Pericles in 1969 and he recalled having recently signed it for a man who'd announced that he hadn't been born when it was taken. Ian drew himself up and – looking taller than he was and rather like *FU* – looked down his nose and pronounced, "What cheek!"

I was surprised to hear him say that he preferred film

and TV work to theatre these days because, 'if you mess it up, you can do it over again.' I don't imagine he messed it up very often. The stage door crowd was great fun, too. I enjoyed hearing Ian's British fans talk about the plays they'd seen him in and how happy they were to see him in Stratford again.

I next saw Ian early in 2004 in Toronto, again in *The Hollow Crown*. There'd been a bit of role-reshuffling and Ian played Charles I and II back to back this time, as he'd done in the '60s. After the first was condemned he stood, head down, half-concealed behind the guitarist, Steven Gray, who sang an air that the king had composed. Song over, Ian came bounding out, picked up the lectern, carried it to centre stage and had us laughing before he'd even opened his mouth.

Ian and Vanessa Redgrave, more than anyone else in the three *Hollow Crown* versions I've seen, seemed to me to embody each of their diverse characters from the moment they started to speak; both actors simply vanished into their roles, whatever the roles might be.

Two other friends, Maree Wilson from Wales and Cindy Brome, also from New York, had come to Toronto. We decided to invite the Richardsons to lunch. None of us knew the city, so when Maroussia offered to make reservations at a restaurant they liked, we happily accepted. They'd rented a gorgeous apartment, high up, with river views. We met Ian in the lobby and he took us up to give us a quick tour before we headed out to a steakhouse.

I was amused and charmed by the way this man, so dominant on stage and screen, relied on his wife in everyday matters. He wanted a steak but didn't know what kind he liked and had to ask her. I'd brought a 1960 production photo from *The Winter's Tale*, the only one I had of them together on stage, Maroussia front and centre, Ian the leftmost of five actors ranged behind her. Maroussia signed her stage name next to her picture, but Ian's flamboyant signature wound up beside Roy Dotrice. Both young actors wore long white beards and I wondered whether Ian's eyesight was so poor that he couldn't tell which one he was, but when I questioned him he explained that he'd wanted to sign near Maroussia. And of course, he grabbed the bill at the end of the meal.

Cindy Brome – Admirer and Friend – recalling some of her favourite scenes

Bill Haydon was an interesting variation on the upper class man raised to rule: the authority, the perfect speech, the intelligence, the education – without humility to temper it – was pure arrogance. Bill Haydon's final interview with George Smiley at the end is a kind of symphony of arrogance, both political and personal. His total lack of remorse, his gentleman's poise, is shocking.

When he says how much he hates America, there's a line, 'The economic repression of the masses, institutionalised.' The pause on the comma, the emphasis he puts on the word "institutionalised" and the disgust with which he enunciates every syllable made me hate America, too, for a moment – and I'm American.

In *The Fourth Protocol (1987)*, Ian had a wonderful scene in which he revealed to a hapless diplomat, played by Anton Rogers, who has unwittingly been passing secrets to the Soviets, not only that he'd been caught, but that he'd been duped by the Russians. He spelled out the whole ghastly thing in a very soft voice, barely above a whisper, sometimes even with a tiny smile. The victim wasn't worth his contempt – he was literally distasteful to Irvine. He reduced the man to a weeping pulp and then gave him an errand to do, like Urquhart did with Roger O'Neill in *House of Cards*.

He didn't move at all. His voice, rising or falling in pitch, was just enough, his pauses, just enough. The quietness of the scene is reminiscent of Urquhart interviewing Sarah Harding (Kitty Aldridge) in *To Play the King*. In both scenes, Ian's soft voice expressed his character's complete authority.

He could use that authority in comedy as well. In *Brazil* (1985), Ian played Mr. Warrenn, the boss of the main character, Sam Lowry, played by Jonathan Pryce. We first glimpsed him as he raced through the rabbit warren of the department followed by a clutch of subordinates, a farcical perpetual motion machine. His decisions came so fast, they became ridiculous. 'Yes! No! Yes, yes, yes!' His vocal skill came into play as he carried on two different lines of conversation at the same time; one with Pryce and the other with several of his supplicants.

In *Blunt* (1985), the story of the notorious traitor Anthony Blunt, an art historian and the 'fourth man' in the 1951 spy scandal, there was a very moving, silent scene. Blunt received a coded message from his lover, Guy Burgess (Anthony Hopkins) that Burgess was unexpectedly defecting to Russia. First shocked, then horrified, Blunt realized that he had to clean out Burgess' apartment to avoid being caught himself.

Desperately scooping up everything there, he breathlessly carried it all to the museum where he lived and worked. Down in the bowels of the building, he proceeded to burn all traces of Burgess in the furnace. As he tossed old postcards and other reminders of their long relationship into the fire, he mourned the one true love of his otherwise icy life. Ian played the whole thing with exquisite, heartbreaking delicacy and completely without sentimentality.

Ian left us a wealth of such moments, rich with humanity and contradictions, which tell us more about ourselves than we might like. He had the actor's version of perfect pitch, able to give passionate, full-blooded performances that never sank into sentimentality or bathos. He used his magnificent acting skills with taste, intelligence and integrity.

In person, Ian was a kind and generous man, with a wonderful sense of humour.

From Hell

In 2001, Ian had a role in the film *From Hell*, about Jack the Ripper. He played Sir Charles Warren, Commissioner of the Metropolitan Police. The film, directed by the Hughes Brothers, starred Johnny Depp as Warren's subordinate, Inspector Abeline, as well as Ian Holm, Robbie Coltrane and Heather Graham.

Ian was delighted that almost all of his scenes in the film were with Johnny Depp, though some were more comfortable than others:

"Johnny is the sweetest, gentlest person I've ever met. I remember, in *From Hell*, he had to attack me. The director came round after the first camera rehearsal and said to him, 'It doesn't look good, Johnny. You've really got to go for Ian and make it look as though you are trying to kill him.' I turned to Johnny and said, 'Come on, just go for it. I've done a lot of Shakespeare plays with swords and battle-axes. I'm used to being beaten about the place.'

So Johnny said, 'Okay.' They went for the take and Johnny went for my throat and I could feel him strangling me and I was thinking, when are they going to say 'cut!' When they did, Johnny looked at me and put his arms around me. This beautiful young man put his arms around this elderly gentleman and said, 'Oh God, have I hurt you, have I hurt you? Are you all right?' And I thought, well now, that's really something."

Strange

Never afraid to try something different, Ian played the mysterious Canon Black in *Strange*, a BBC Sci Fi pilot episode and six-part series. *Strange*, which starred Richard Coyle and Samantha Janus, gave Ian the opportunity to take things a bit easier, but still walk in and steal his scenes.

Debbie Moon, reviewing the series in *The Zone*, commented, "every supernatural drama needs a villain and *Strange*'s trump card is Ian Richardson, as the villainous Canon Black. Witheringly sarcastic, coolly malevolent, Richardson plays all the ambiguities of a role that often leaves you unsure whether Black is simply a bitter old man opposing Strange out of personal dislike, or the Devil himself."

12

The Curtain Comes Down whilst the Applause is Still Ringing

Hogfather

"It could only have been the irreplaceable Ian Richardson. His was the first and the only name on my list." Thus director Vadim Jean describes the response of Terry Pratchett, speaking at the London Institute of Education, long before a Discworld novel was adapted for the screen and the first time Vadim saw Pratchett in the flesh. The question he had posed was which living actor the legendary author felt would best bring Death to life.

Ian provided both the voice of Death, a much-loved character from Terry Pratchett's Discworld novels, and the narration for the adaptation of *Hogfather*. Pratchett aficionados had very definite ideas of what their image of Discworld and its characters were. One Internet Movie Database User commented, "I didn't think anyone could do a better job with THE VOICE than Christopher Lee in the 1990's cartoon series of *Soul Music*, but I was proved wrong when Ian Richardson triumphed in both gravitas and endearment."

In his review in *Dreamwatch Presents Total Sci Fi*, James Skipp commenting on Ian's role said, "Droll, sympathetic and ham-free, this Grim Reaper is an utter joy."

Vadim Jean – Director

He was the first. What I would have done if he'd said 'no' I really can't imagine. But he did say 'yes' and so I had the joy and privilege of working with one of those actors you dream of working with. It was just as well Ian Richardson agreed to being the voice of Death in Terry Pratchett's *Hogfather*, because his name wasn't just the first name on the list – it was the only one.

On my first film, *Leon the Pig Farmer*, it had been Mark Frankel. In my experience, when the first name on the cast list agrees to play the first role you offer to anyone, it's usually a good omen. With Ian and *Hogfather* I like to think it was a wonderful one.

It is a tribute to Ian that at the point I asked him, we were still in the very earliest stages of development. All we had was some test footage and half a script. He agreed to lend us his unique voice for the show reel that would eventually land us the finance for the film itself. He believed in it right from the start and continued to do so, even after the fourth recording session.

I first became aware of Ian when I was still at school. The only actor I knew was my mother's goddaughter, Kim Hicks, and her first big break was in *The Master of Ballantrae* for ITV, playing opposite... yes, Ian. He flogged her from his horse, I vaguely remember. But the thing was – someone I knew had actually been in a film with someone famous.

And then of course inevitably, there was *House of Cards*. Death in Discworld rather likes humans so it was not just the ominous tones of a grim reaper that

Ian as 'FU' - Francis Urquhart

The 'Macbeths' - Ian and Diane Fletcher as Francis and Elizabeth Urquhart

'FU' and Mattie - Ian with Susannah Harker

Catherine the Great
with Brian Blessed

With Nickolas Grace and Isla Blair
in *The Final Cut*

As Harpagon, with Ben Miles, in *The Miser* at the Chichester Festival Theatre, 1995

The Chichester dressing room, October, 1997

The Author with Ian and Maroussia in the dressing room, Savoy Theatre, March 1998

With Paul Marcus and Charles Edwards on the *Murder Rooms* set

Posing as a blind beggar for *The Kingdom of Bones*

Winner of a Sherlock Holmes Award for his portrayal as Joseph Bell

In *From Hell,* with Johnny Depp and Robbie Coltrane

Ian and Maroussia with Sadie and Eddie Mail, Alveston Manor, Stratford, 2002

Ian and Maroussia, Stratford dressing room, 2002

Toga fitting for *Imperium: Nero*

With Donald Sinden, Diana Rigg and Derek Jacobi in Sydney for the first *Hollow Crown* tour

With Maroussia in Toronto for *The Hollow Crown*, 2004
© Anne Gilhuly

With Juliet Stevenson at the Cheltenham Literature Festival, 2004
© Anne Gilhuly

In *Becoming Jane*, with
James McAvoy

Photo taken in 2006
© Jeremy Richardson

As Edward Kimberley in
The Creeper

Ian's voice so mellifluously brought to the performance but also his dry warmth. And so it was impossible to resist adapting the completely in character Urquhart line, 'You might think that...' for Death. Ian was very patient with me... He was even patient with me beyond Take Two, which he told me was always somehow his best performance.

However, even more memorable for me in his canon of work was *Porterhouse Blue*. There was a mini golden age of drama around that period with things like *Edge of Darkness* and *A Very British Coup*, all dramas that inspired me at the end of my time at university to think about becoming a film maker. But the one that stayed with me most was the Tom Sharpe. The humour (and not just the cartoonish covers) shared by those novels and Pratchett's in the '80's, perhaps struck a chord. Whatever, the thought of reuniting Ian and David Jason as Death's manservant Albert was too tempting and, once we had the green light for *Hogfather*, happily we were able to do so.

They never met on set as 6'7" Dutchman, Marnix van der Broek, marvellously wears the mask, robe and wields the scythe in *Hogfather*, miming to Ian's voice, together bringing life to Death; but to see the warmth of Ian and David's meeting again at the premiere was a wonderful moment.

I was actually seated at my desk writing *The Colour of Magic* when I heard the news of Ian's passing. He will of course always be what we call a 'Pratchett player.' But I also thought it would be fitting for his son Miles to continue the family's involvement and cast him as Zlorf, the head of the Assassin's Guild, in *The Colour of Magic*. Somebody had of course to stand in for Ian as the voice of Death and it was gratifying to hear from Miles that Ian would be pleased that it was his great friend Christopher Lee taking up the mantle.

The Creeper

I saw Ian performing in the revival of the Pauline Macauley's 1960's play, *The Creeper*, directed by Bill Bryden. Ian played the main role, Edward Kimberley, an eccentric millionaire. It was a lovely part for him and he was well supported by the rest of the cast, Alan Cox, Oliver Dimsdale, Robert Styles and Harry Towb.

It was a joy to see Ian, who became like an adoptive uncle to the younger actors, particularly on tour. He was in good form and his dressing rooms were such happy places after the performances.

John Thaxter, writing in *The Stage*, 1 September, 2005, said, "It provides a gift of a part for the distinguished Ian Richardson, who invests the role with his prowling presence and deliciously cool irony, retaining his dignity even while dancing the light fantastic, playing with a Hornby train set in stationmaster guise, or donning Hiawatha headgear for bow and arrow games."

Bronagh Taggart, reviewing the play in the *British Theatre Guide*, noted, "Richardson, who has been absent from the West End for eight years, was in fine form. He played the comic moments to the hilt, yet he still had the ability to move us by his vulnerability in a rather under-written part."

However, after a successful provincial tour and transfer to the Playhouse Theatre in the West End in February, 2006, critics slated the play as being 'old fashioned'. Some of them even condemned Ian for undertaking it rather than returning to a Shakespearian role.

The adverse publicity meant that *The Creeper* closed early, and Ian announced his retirement from the theatre.

Alan Cox – Actor, Michael

I went with my sister and my Dad [actor Brian Cox] for a family outing to The Savoy and saw Ian in *The Magistrate*. It was just such a joy to watch him work. When the opportunity arose to work with him I

jumped at it. I almost didn't care what the play was –
I knew my reasons for doing it and enjoyed it.

When we were rehearsing *The Creeper*, Ian knew his
lines and was off-book by the read-through. I
remember coming in one day – I used to cycle in –
and I was wheeling my bike into the church hall we
were using. He was walking through his stuff with
Oliver and completely precise and detailed and was
working very hard. Without missing a beat he said,
"And then I come over here and, ah, Michel [one of
Edward's affectations was to call Michael 'Michel']
comes in," without actually saying, 'good morning',
because he was so in the zone. Ollie winked at me and
I winked back at him and Ian spun round and said,
"Are you two sending me up?" I just said, "No, Ian,
I'm still on the Harrow Road and not really in the room
yet," and we carried on.

In the coffee break he came up to Ollie and me and
put us in a headlock and said, "The three of us have to
be the best of friends or else we're fucked. I can be an
awful bully sometimes and if I'm doing anything that
is annoying you, you must tell me straight away and
not let it turn into resentment," which was fantastic.

The experiences and backgrounds of Ollie and I were
very different to Ian's. He was part of a generation
that learnt their craft doing weekly rep and that way
of working sometimes feels a little old school. I
remember saying to Ollie that it may be old school but
it was a school and there was a lot to learn from it.
And he was fantastic – the way he orchestrated his
phrasing, the way he mapped out his business and
how he delivered great long swathes of text in one
breath was wonderful to observe and work alongside.

He was incredibly generous on stage. If he, as all
actors do, came in too early or fluffed a line, he had

this thing of almost apologising with his face for treading on your toes.

Ian had worked with my Dad before [in *A Cotswold Death*] and they were both Scots and had got on very well and he was quite paternal towards me and very supportive. He used to lend me DVDs of his early work and I watched the whole of *Mountbatten: The Last Viceroy* and then *Private Schulz* and he was just terrific in that – so funny.

In one of the performances, he had laryngitis and after the curtain call he went to the front of the stage and said, "Ladies and gentlemen, I'd just like to thank you for putting up with my laryngitis," and he got a huge round of applause.

A friend of mine was a teacher at Guildford Drama School and when the houses were very thin at the Playhouse I said to him, "I can get you tickets, why don't you send some of your students down?" About twenty of them came to see the show and after the matinee I showed them around the set and Ian popped down and sat with them and just told them stories and was utterly enchanting. Normally he had a lie-down between performances and to forego that to chat with them was very gracious of him.

———

James Cellan Jones

The last time I saw Ian was in *The Creeper* in the West End. His was a marvellous performance and he really got hold of the play and bonded the cast together.

———

Sam Farr – Photographer

I last photographed Ian for the *Bath Chronicle* in September, 2005, at the Theatre Royal, where he was starring in *The Creeper*.

Ian was a true gentleman and was always keen to help. He held the reflector for the photographers while we took photos of his co-star, Oliver Dimsdale.

As my wife, Wendy, is a great fan of *House of Cards*, I dropped a picture back for him to sign for her. To her surprise and delight, he took it to her work and delivered it in person. He then posted us a handwritten note of thanks for the prints I sent him.

Cindy Lou Fiorina – Admirer and Friend

The last time I saw Ian was in September 2005, when I went to Windsor to see *The Creeper*. The show was a *tour de force* for the range of Ian's talents. I was not to know that would be the last time I'd ever see him, so I cherish even more my memories of that magical visit.

The trip also included lunch hosted by Ian and Maroussia, with several other mutual friends present. The charm and wit Ian exhibited ensured there was never a dull moment. He loved an audience, especially an all-female one, even though he protested that we would all gang up on him. After the evening performance I attended a reception in the theatre bar and, with the champagne flowing, Ian once again had us eagerly listening to him with amusement and pleasure. He was the perfect host and a true gentleman. And one of the finest men I've ever known.

The Alchemist

After the disappointment of *The Creeper*, the news that Ian had reversed his decision to retire from the theatre and accept Nicholas Hytner's invitation to appear in Ben Jonson's *The Alchemist* at the Olivier Theatre was greeted with great joy and relief.

His last theatrical performance was a triumph.

Writing in *The Observer*, 17 September, 2006, Susannah Clapp said, "As the luxurious hedonist Epicure Mammon, Ian Richardson has several of the most sumptuous of 17th-century speeches. He delivers a discourse on his future happiness which talks of his 'tongues of carps, dormice, and camels' heels' in the tones of a telly gourmet'. Startlingly – these are stop-the-show arias – he drops the speeches with restraint, never over-egging the plush vocabulary, but allowing each over-fruity phrase to speak for itself. And then, right at the end, reaching his apogee, he allows a moment of excess, in one long warbling sigh."

Alastair Macauley, writing in the *Financial Times* in September, 2006 struggled at times with the enunciation of some, but noted, "Ian Richardson, by contrast, is a paragon of clarity as Sir Epicure Mammon, his sense of the verse's pulse is superlative and he seems refreshed by playing for once a character who is a fool. The languor with which he voices a corrupt fantasy, 'naked amid my succubi', made me long to see him as Malvolio."

In the *Daily Mail* on 15 September, 2006, Quentin Letts commented, "the greatest revelation of the night comes from Ian Richardson as rich Sir Epicure Mammon. Wigged so that he resembles Sir John Harvey-Jones, he is the embodiment of pink-fripperied foolishness, of aging vanity and florid, crooning greed."

Nicholas Hytner – Director

My earliest memories as a serious theatre-goer are dominated by Ian Richardson's incandescent performances for the RSC in the late 60's and early 70's. I was first taken to Stratford by my parents and then went regularly on school trips.

There must be tens of thousands whose attachment to Shakespeare was established by the clarity, wit, passion and charisma of Ian's Angelo, Coriolanus, Richard II, Berowne and Prospero. I have a horrible feeling that *Richard III* will always seem to be about Buckingham to me, as Ian effortlessly pulled the focus of that play to the King's co-conspirator, not by hogging the limelight, but simply by being more interesting than anyone else.

It was a burning ambition of mine to work with him and it delighted me more than I can say that he agreed to make his National Theatre debut as Sir Epicure Mammon in *The Alchemist* at the end of 2006. He brought to us all the gifts that made him one of the greatest of all classical actors and one of the funniest. That he was dazzling in the part was no surprise.

What touched me so deeply was the unalloyed delight he took in the performances of Alex Jennings and Simon Russell Beale. Sir Epicure Mammon provides a magnificent still centre to scenes in which the two conmen Subtle and Face run hyperactive rings around their victim. They are the kind of parts that Ian did better than anyone else. Ian was thrilled by the invention and speed of Simon and Alex and took huge pleasure in apparently feeding them. The result, of course, was that you couldn't take your eyes off him.

It grieves me profoundly that his National Theatre debut was his last stage performance.

Alex Jennings – Face

I was a huge admirer of Ian from when I saw him with the Prospect Theatre Company in *Romeo and Juliet* and *The Government Inspector*. I remember *The Government Inspector* particularly because he was magnetic and electrifying as a stage actor.

Seeing him on screen was wonderful, particularly in *House of Cards* and *Tinker Tailor*. He was such a master and had such a love of acting that was infectious. He was completely in it but you could tell that he was having a good time. *House of Cards* was just astonishing – wonderful to see and it was inspiring to witness someone so revered as a stage actor having that kind of success on a wider field.

I remember when Nick phoned me up and told me we had Ian Richardson. I couldn't believe it – it was like a great big present. There was a real sense of excitement here.

He was such a delight to work with and in rehearsals he was so open to a new way of approaching classical work. There was a point where he spotted that the way we were doing it was perhaps a bit less full and he completely adjusted and slipped into doing something a bit more naturalistic. It was a joy to watch. I used to listen to him every night and loved what he did with the language.

He was so supportive of what Simon and I were doing and seemed to enjoy it and it was such a giggle. And we were so aware that we were working with a thoroughbred. I feel so grateful that I got to work with him, because he was a real idol.

What struck me most was watching him get to grips with the great big set piece that part is, adjusting his performance and not being as florid as could have been – and it would have been brilliant – but bringing it down and making it very true and real and human and touching. And how hard he worked at that and how challenged he was by it and yet still loving the process. He had a brilliant way with language – phrasing it and landing on words and giving them a ping.

I do some work for Cancer UK and bi-annually they have a Carol Concert at Saint Paul's. I was asked by the events committee to approach Ian to take part. He was absolutely happy to do that and he read the lesson and opened the proceedings. My partner said that it was like there was suddenly a Rolls Royce driving down the centre aisles of St Paul's Cathedral and it was the voice of God. It was extraordinary what he did – in really difficult acoustics – but he knew just how to do it.

—◆◆◆—

Anne Gilhuly – Admirer and Friend

I was so pleased, especially after *The Creeper*, that *The Alchemist*, Ian's last play, was such a great success.

For a man over 70, Ian was astonishingly limber. He got one of the biggest laughs of the evening as Sir Epicure Mammon tried to impress a young widow by swinging his leg over a chair before sitting down. He got an even bigger laugh when he clutched his back and made a horrible face.

We met for drinks one night after the show and Robin Weatherall, a former RSC musician who'd toured with Ian in the '60's, turned up with a busload of St Louisans. Ian had been his best man when he'd married a girl from Omaha, but they hadn't seen each other in decades. They reminisced.

Miles was with the RSC at the time and I told his parents he'd impressed me in *Henry VI*. It was a small role but he had a big presence and a gorgeous voice and reminded me a lot of his Dad. Ian recalled that Miles was appearing in *As You Like It* during *The Creeper's* West End run, playing Le Beau and understudying Jacques, as Ian had done some 40 years earlier. Quite by chance, he went on as Jacques on the day his parents went to see him. Ian played the proud father for laughs, telling us that when Miles came to 'All the world's a stage,' he'd felt like standing up and telling everyone in the theatre, 'That's my boy!' And he pounded on his leg, glowing.

———

Shadowlands

One of Ian's final recordings, was the radio broadcast of the adaptation of Brian Sibley's book *Shadowlands* about the love story between C S Lewis and Joy Davidman.

———

Brian Sibley – Writer

"He was our one and only choice for the role…" That has become the everyday cliché by which people describe the casting of any star in a play or film.

In this instance, however, it was absolutely true. When BBC Radio 2 commissioned a serialised reading of my book *Shadowlands*, my producer Malcolm Prince and I sat down to discuss who might be asked to read the book and we both said one name – Ian Richardson.

First published in 1985, *Shadowlands* is the story of C S Lewis, Oxford academic and author of *The Chronicles of Narnia*, and of his late-flowering love for the American writer, Joy Davidman, whom he eventually lost to cancer. It was a play on TV and stage and, later, a feature film.

To present the book in its new form, as eight 15-minute weekly broadcasts, I decided not simply to abridge, but to restructure the material completely and it was this version, together with a copy of the original book, which was sent to Ian via his agent.

There was a rather worrying period while we awaited a response that didn't come. Then, after several weeks of silence, we got word that Ian had agreed to read the book and we were thrilled – although just a little anxious at the prospect of working with the man who created the terrifying persona of Francis Urquhart!

Of course, it turned out to be a blissfully happy experience and we could not have been better served. Ian arrived early and worked flat out for seven hours at a demanding and completely unrelenting pace.

At one point in what was a long day of intensely focused concentration, Malcolm – sensitive to the possibility that Ian might be getting tired – suggested that we might complete the recording on another day. But Ian wouldn't hear of it.

Refusing any refreshment (other than water) he steamed ahead at full force until he had completed the recording of all eight programmes – *and* re-recorded the *first* one because, having reached the end, he was dissatisfied with the manner in which he had begun and wanted to redo the opening.

A few weeks later, when we heard the tragic news of Ian's death, it was impossible not to reflect on the fact that if we had scheduled another recording date, the project might never have been completed.

Ian came to the work fully prepared: Maroussia had provided him with phonetic pronunciations for all the place names referred to in the episode in which Jack took Joy on a final holiday to Greece and Ian had clearly given a lot of thought to the changing moods of the piece from episode to episode and how most effectively to portray the central characters.

Despite this preparation, he invited criticism and delighted in being given notes. When I first dared to suggest a particular approach to a passage, he immediately responded, "Yes, yes! I understand. Thank you. I *love* taking direction!"

Peter Hall has suggested that Ian always listened courteously to his director, but ultimately did his 'own thing'. With this project, on the contrary, he was very concerned to hear and take on board any thoughts or suggestions that Malcolm and I had to offer.

When I was bold enough to propose a way of reading one of C S Lewis' poems, he immediately took the note, saying, "Of course! I see *exactly* how it should be. You know, I learnt to speak verse under John Barton – I shudder to think what *he* would have said." A particular retake that perfectly demonstrated his ability to seize on a meaning and to make it work to perfection occurred in the penultimate episode that dealt with Joy's last days.

When Joy dies, the text reads: 'She smiled,' said Jack, 'but not at me.' Ian read this line with a sad, dying fall to his voice. It was extremely poignant, but, after a moment's hesitation, I suggested that Jack Lewis might have drawn reassurance from Joy's smile so that, whilst it may not have been for him, it was an acknowledgement that Joy had become suddenly aware of something beyond death.

Ian instantly seized on this thought and gave it that hopeful, upbeat interpretation and turned a simple phrase into one carrying a wealth of meaning and a depth of feeling.

Of course, any direction offered by Malcolm Prince or myself was minimal. What could we ever truly tell an actor with Ian's prodigious talent and years of experience?

Watching him at work, as he grappled with the emotions underpinning the story and in particular the sense of overwhelming grief, giving way to slowly emerging hope that is at the heart of *Shadowlands*, was a privilege.

Before, between and after the recording there was some excellent chat: shared thoughts about the stories of Saki, which he had just finished recording, about the work of Mervyn Peake and about our mutual friend, Christopher Lee, whom he had first met during the filming of *Gormenghast*.

Ian also recalled his first brush with the work of C S Lewis when he had read *The Lion, the Witch and the Wardrobe* as an audio book and of the experience of recording Lewis' *The Screwtape Letters*, the broadcasts of which had been avidly followed and commented on by various members of the clergy whom he encountered.

An episode in *Shadowlands* describing how, while in Greece, Joy Davidman had forced herself – despite serious difficulties with walking – to scramble to the top of the Acropolis, prompted Ian to share a memory of his and Maroussia's visit to Sicily, in the mid-90's.

At the top of Mount Etna, he had met a woman who, whilst seriously disabled and clearly on borrowed time, had stoically struggled to the very rim of the volcano, resolutely determined not to miss a moment of the experience of being there.

When the recordings were complete, we parted and I determined to find another opportunity to work with Ian. It was not to be, but the fact that the series was still being broadcast only a few days after the service of thanksgiving for Ian's life, was a reminder that, like all great performers, his work lives on.

Sadness at his passing was inevitable, but Ian was a man of faith and, as he had read in the final episode of my abridgement, the Shadowlands had now been left behind... 'The term is over,' Lewis wrote, 'the holidays have begun. The dream is ended: this is the morning.'

One last, enjoyable memory from a memorable day: after several noisy outbursts from people in the corridor outside the studio that had interrupted the recording, someone walked by whistling merrily. Ian got up from the microphone, went to the door and pointed out to the whistler that a red light was illuminated over the door indicating that a recording was in progress.

When he returned to his seat, producer Malcolm Prince apologized on behalf of a thoughtless colleague. "Oh, that's alright," replied Ian, "I don't think he'll do it again – I gave him one of my best Francis Urquhart looks!"

13

"And Farewell King"

In the final weeks of his life, Ian's acting duties were devoted to various recordings. As well as *Shadowlands*, he played the Oxford historian A L Rowse in *Accolades*, the BBC Radio 4 drama written by Christopher William Hill, and recorded *The Chronicles of Clovis*, by Saki, for Silksoundbooks.

Accolades was broadcast shortly after Ian's death and David Sexton, writing in the *Sunday Telegraph* on 11 March, 2007, said, "As Rowse – camp, affected, phonily precise, utterly deranged by vanity – Richardson couldn't have been bettered."

How appropriate that these last projects were all audio works. Ian was undoubtedly an exceptional all-round actor but his greatest, most glorious gift was his voice. And in each of these recordings, the performances were as outstanding as any given earlier in his career.

A month after his passing, the release of the film *Becoming Jane* presented audiences with an opportunity to see his final screen performance. The film told of the supposed romance between novelist Jane Austen, played by Anne Hathaway, and Irishman Tom Lefroy, played by James McAvoy. Ian played Lefroy's uncle, Judge Langlois.

The *indieLONDON* review said, "the film is notable for featuring the last big screen performance from the late Ian Richardson, as Tom's disapproving mentor, and succeeds in providing a significant reminder of his immense talent." Derek

Elley, writing in *Variety*, 8 March, 2007, noted that, "Ian Richardson brings some dramatic heft to Judge Langlois, Tom's stern uncle-cum-employer." Others described his performance as 'scene-stealing'.

On Thursday, 8 February, 2007, Ian had a wig and costume fitting, ready to start filming a role the following week for an episode of the popular ITV drama series, *Midsomer Murders*. He was in excellent spirits and he and Maroussia were talking about having a belated celebration for their 46th wedding anniversary, which had been on 2 February. He went to bed that night never to wake up, slipping away in the early hours of the following morning. He had a heart condition, which had probably remained undetected for some time, and died of left ventricular failure.

Sir Ian McKellen – 10 February, 2007

In 1989, the Royal Shakespeare Company actors were rehearsing Trevor Nunn's production of *Othello* in a church hall in London when the news reached us that Laurence Olivier had died. The greatest theatre man of our time was gone. The curtain had fallen. It seemed heartless to proceed, particularly with a play that Olivier had triumphed in, so we abandoned rehearsals as Trevor and I went off to record our tributes for BBC.

I remembered this yesterday afternoon, with more bad news at rehearsals, again with Trevor and the RSC. We were discussing the storm scenes in *King Lear*. Jonathan Hyde blurted out that his wife had just phoned to say Ian Richardson had died in his sleep, aged 72. It seemed incredible. I had seen him so recently onstage, gloriously strutting as Epicure Mammon in the National Theatre's *The Alchemist*.

Trevor reminisced about his first major production for the RSC, *The Revenger's Tragedy*, with Richardson starring as Vendice. This was but one of a string of dramatic villains which culminated, as far as the general public is concerned, on television, with his dastardly Urquhart, the Prime Minister in Michael Dobbs' *House of Cards*.

The utter suddenness of Ian's passing was a terrible shock but it is a blessing that he died so peacefully. He always said that he intended to go before Maroussia because he couldn't contemplate life without her, so he had his wish. And he always used to say that the curtain should come down whilst the applause is still ringing. That was certainly the case with his career, his final performances being excellent and showing no diminution of his peerless talents.

On 15 May, 2007, a service celebrating Ian's life was held in a packed St Paul's Church in Covent Garden. Tributes were paid by sons Jeremy and Miles and by Sir Peter Hall and there were readings and performances by Helen Mirren, Simon Russell Beale, Richard Pasco, Derek Jacobi, Donald Sinden, Isobel Buchanan, Guy Woolfenden and Stephen Gray.

The service was organised by Maroussia, who by this time had returned to the acting career she had put on hold for so many years to bring up the boys and give constant support to Ian. Ian had always complimented Maroussia's taste and it could be evidenced by the poem she chose for Helen Mirren to read – *Dirge Without Music*, by Edna St Vincent Millay.

'The answers quick and keen, the honest look, the laughter, the love,
They are gone. They have gone to feed the roses. Elegant and curled
Is the blossom. Fragrant is the blossom. I know. But I do not approve.
More precious was the light in your eyes than all the roses in the
world.'

The rendition of that remarkable verse in particular provided a profoundly moving and indelible moment for all present.

The last time I saw Ian was at the National Theatre on the 13 November, 2006. That evening, he was giving a Platform talk before the performance of *The Alchemist*. Typically of Ian, he hadn't expected many people to turn up for the talk, but the theatre was packed. And he was as entertaining, forthright and self-effacing as ever.

After the play, I had a quick drink with Ian, Maroussia and Louise Plaschkes, widow of Otto Plaschkes, who had produced the two Sherlock Holmes films Ian had starred in. I had to rush off to catch the sleeper back to Glasgow and went to say 'cheerio' to Ian who was, by this time, along with his agent, Jean Diamond, ordering a fresh round of drinks at the bar.

Ian had had problems with his knees and hip for some time and after exchanging a hug and a kiss, I patted him and said to him, "For goodness sake, get your knees seen to."

Little did I know that it was his heart rather than his joints which was failing him and that I would never see him again, nor experience a room or stage lighting up when he strode in.

Ian was hugely respected, both as an actor and as a person and touched the lives of so many. He had a vast talent, coupled with thorough professionalism and an exemplary work ethic, and made an impact with every performance he gave. For all his accomplishments, he was a modest man who had a unique way of letting people into his life and extending the hand of friendship to them.

Postscript

In November, 2008, Maroussia and Miles placed Ian's ashes into the foundations beneath what will be the front row of the stalls of the rebuilt Royal Shakespeare Theatre in Stratford-upon-Avon, which is due to re-open in 2010. I can't think of a more touching or suitable resting place.

Performances

Plays

Year	Production	Company/Theatre	Role
1956	Julius Caesar	Citizens Theatre	
1956	Richard II	Citizens Theatre	
1957	Hedda Gabler	Her Majesty's, Carlisle	
1957	Sailor Beware	Her Majesty's, Carlisle	
1958	The Lovebirds	Her Majesty's, Carlisle	Victor Sellars
1958	Plaintiff in a Pretty Hat	Her Majesty's, Carlisle	Watkyn
1958	Three Elizabethan Rarities	Birmingham Rep	
1958	A Dead Secret	Birmingham Rep	
1958	Fear Came to Supper	Birmingham Rep	Andrei
1958	The Importance of Being Earnest	Birmingham Rep	Jack Worthing
1958	The Royal Astrologers	Birmingham Rep	First Thief
1958	The Creditors	Birmingham Rep	Adolph
1959	The Long and the Short and the Tall	Birmingham Rep	Private Whitaker
1959	The Duenna	Birmingham Rep	Don Ferdinand
1959	Who's Who	Birmingham Rep	Newsreaders
1959	Gammer Gurton's Needle	Birmingham Rep	Dr Rat, The Curate
1959	Fratricide Punished	Birmingham Rep	Francisco
1959	Johan Johan	Birmingham Rep	
1959	A Yorkshire Tragedy	Birmingham Rep	
1959	Hamlet	Birmingham Rep	Hamlet
1959	The Enchanted Forest	Birmingham Rep	Oberon (also wrote the music)

1960	The Merchant of Venice	RSC		Prince of Arragon
1960	The Two Gentlemen of Verona	RSC		Thurio
1960	Twelfth Night	RSC		Sir Andrew Aguecheek
1960	The Taming of the Shrew	RSC		Lord
1960	The Winter's Tale	RSC		Old Gentleman 2
1960	The Duchess of Malfi	RSC		Count Malatesti
1961	Hamlet	RSC		Guildenstern
1961	Much Ado About Nothing	RSC		Don John
1961	Richard III	RSC		Sir William Catesby
1961	As You Like it	RSC		Le Beau/Jaques
1962	Measure for Measure	RSC		Lucio
1962	A Midsummer Night's Dream	RSC		Oberon
1962	The Taming of the Shrew	RSC		Tranio
1962	Macbeth	RSC		Seyton
1962	Cymbeline	RSC		Lord
1962	The Comedy of Errors	RSC		Antipholus of Ephesus
1962	Dr Faustus	RSC		Old Man
1963	A Midsummer Night's Dream	RSC		Oberon
1963	The Representative	RSC		Doctor
1963	The Miracles	Southwark Cathedral		Herod
1964	King Lear	RSC		Edmund
1964	Marat/Sade	RSC		Herald
1964	The Jew of Malta	RSC		Ithamore/Machiavel
1964	The Merry Wives of Windsor	RSC		Frank Ford
1965	The Comedy of Errors	RSC		Antipholus of Syracuse
1965	Squire Puntila & His Servant Matti	RSC		Eino Silakka
1965	Marat/Sade	RSC		Marat
1966	Henry V	RSC		Chorus
1966	The Revenger's Tragedy	RSC		Vendice
1967	Coriolanus	RSC		Coriolanus
1968	All's Well That Ends Well	RSC		Bertram
1968	Macbeth	RSC		Malcolm
1968	Julius Caesar	RSC		Cassius
1968	The Merry Wives of Windsor	RSC		Frank Ford
1969	Pericles	RSC		Pericles
1969	The Revenger's Tragedy	RSC		Vendice

Year	Play	Company/Theatre	Role
1970	Measure for Measure	RSC	Angelo
1970	Richard III	RSC	Duke of Buckingham
1970	The Two Gentlemen of Verona	RSC	Proteus
1970	The Tempest	RSC	Prospero
1972	Trelawny of the Wells	Bristol Old Vic	Tom Wrench
1973	Love's Labour's Lost	RSC	Berowne
1974	Richard II	RSC	Richard II/Bolingbroke
1974	Summerfolk	RSC	Shalimov
1974	The Marquis of Keith	RSC	Scholz
1974	Cymbeline	RSC	Iachimo
1975	Love's Labour's Lost	RSC	Berowne
1975	The Merry Wives of Windsor	RSC	Frank Ford
1975	Richard III	RSC	Richard III
1976	My Fair Lady	St James/Lunt-Fontanne Theatres, Broadway	Henry Higgins
1977	Man and Superman	Shaw Festival Theatre, Stratford, Ontario	Jack Tanner
1977	The Millionairess	Shaw Festival Theatre, Stratford, Ontario	The Doctor
1979	The Government Inspector	Bristol Old Vic	Khlestakov
1979	Romeo and Juliet	Bristol Old Vic	Mercutio
1981	Lolita	Brooks Addison Theatre, Broadway	A Certain Gentleman
1995	The Miser	Chichester Festival Theatre	Harpagon
1997	The Magistrate	Chichester Festival Theatre/Savoy Theatre	Aeneas Posket
2005/ 2006	The Creeper	On Tour/ Playhouse Theatre	Edward Kimberley
2006	The Alchemist	National Theatre	Sir Epicure Mammon

Recitals

1960s/1970s	The Hollow Crown	RSC	Performer
1968 & 1997	Pleasure & Repentance	RSC	Performer
1979	He That Plays the King	RSC	Deviser & Performer
1999	The Seven Ages of Man	Yvonne Arnaud Theatre, Guildford	Solo Performer
2002/2003	The Hollow Crown	RSC – Australia & New Zealand/ Stratford	Performer
2003/2004	Fond & Familiar	Winchester/ Berkhamsted	Performer
2004	The Hollow Crown	RSC – Princess of Wales Theatre, Toronto	Performer

Television Work

Year	Programme	Role
1963	As You Like It	Le Beau
1964	The Comedy of Errors	Antipholus of Ephesus
1967	Horizon – Dynamo, the Life of Michael Faraday	Michael Faraday
1968	All's Well That Ends Well	Bertram
1969	A Voyage Round My Father	The Son
1969	The Canterbury Tales	Death & The Apothecary
1971	Eyeless in Gaza	Anthony Beavis
1973	Gawain and the Green Knight	Narrator
1978	Danton's Death	Robespierre
1978	Play for Today – Sorry (Private View)	Michael
1979	Churchill & The Generals	General Bernard Montgomery
1979	Ike	Field Marshall Montgomery
1979	Tinker Tailor Soldier Spy	Bill Haydon
1980	Gauguin the Savage	Degas
1981	Private Schulz	Major Neuheim/ Melfort/Stanley Kemp/ Steward

1981	Play for Today – A Cotswold Death	Inspector Anthony Arrowsmith
1981	BBC2 Playhouse – Passing Through	Richard
1981	The Woman in White	Frederick Fairlie
1982	Russian Night…1941	Tveritinov
1983	Kisch-Kisch	David
1983	Beauty & The Beast	Father
1983	Salad Days	Various
1983	Number Ten – Underdog	James Ramsay MacDonald
1984	Six Centuries of Verse	
1984	Mistral's Daughter	Adrien Avigdor
1984	The Master of Ballantrae	Mr MacKellar
1984	Brass	Marshall Snelgrove QC
1985	Star Quality	Ray Malcolm
1985	Blunt (The Fourth Man)	Anthony Blunt
1986	Mountbatten: The Last Viceroy	Jawaharlal Nehru
1987	Great Performances – Monsignor Quixote	Bishop of Motopo
1988	Troubles	Edward Spencer
1989	Chillers – Under a Dark Angel's Eye	Lee Maneville
1989	Pursuit (A Twist of Fate)	Doctor Schlossberg
1990	The Plot to Kill Hitler	General Beck
1990	The Winslow Boy	Sir Robert Morton
1990	The Phantom of the Opera	Cholet
1990	The Gravy Train	Michael Spearpoint
1990	House of Cards	Francis Urquhart
1991	The Gravy Train Goes East	Michael Spearpoint
1992	An Ungentlemanly Act	Governor Rex Hunt
1993	Foreign Affairs	Edwin
1993	Remember	Philip Rawlings
1993	To Play the King	Francis Urquhart
1994	A Change of Place	Henri Chambertin
1995	Savage Play	The Earl
1995	Catherine the Great	Count Vorontzov
1995	The Final Cut	Francis Urquhart
1996	The Treasure Seekers	Haig
1996	A Royal Scandal	Narrator
1997	The Woman in White	Frederick Fairlie
1997	The Canterville Ghost	Sir Simon de Canterville
1997	Highlander – Sins of the Father	Max Leiner
1998	A Knight in Camelot	Merlin
1998	Alice Through the Looking Glass	Wasp
1999	The Magician's House	Stephen Tyler

2000	The Magician's House II	Stephen Tyler
2000	Murder Rooms: The Dark Beginnings of Sherlock Holmes	Dr Joseph Bell
2000	Gormenghast	Lord Groan
2001	Murder Rooms (4 Stories)	Dr Joseph Bell
2003	Strange	Canon Black
2004	Daemos Rising	Narrator
2004	Imperium: Nerone	Septimus
2004	Marple: The Body in the Library	Conway Jefferson
2005	Bleak House	Chancellor
2005	Booze Cruise II: The Treasure Hunt	Marcus Foster
2006	Booze Cruise III: The Scattering	Marcus Foster
2006	Hogfather	Death (voice)/Narrator

Films

Year	Film	Role
1967	Marat/Sade	Jean-Paul Marat
1968	A Midsummer Night's Dream	Oberon
1972	The Darwin Adventure	Captain Fitzroy
1972	Man of La Mancha	Padre
1980	Gaugin the Savage	Degas
1982	The Sign of Four	Sherlock Holmes
1982	The Hound of the Baskervilles	Sherlock Holmes
1985	Brazil	Mr Warrenn
1986	Whoops Apocalypse	Rear Admiral Bendish
1987	The Fourth Protocol	Sir Nigel Irvine
1987	Cry Freedom	State Prosecutor
1988	Burning Secret	Mr Tuchman
1989	King of the Wind	Dey of Tunis
1990	Rosencrantz & Guildenstern are Dead	Polonius
1992	Year of the Comet	Sir Mason Harwood
1993	Dirty Weekend	Nimrod
1993	M. Butterfly	Ambassador Toulon
1994	Words Upon the Window Pane	Dr Trench
1997	B*A*P*S	Manley
1997	The Fifth Province	Dr Drudy
1997	Incognito	Turley
1998	Dark City	Mr Book
1999	The King and I	Kralahome (voice)
2000	102 Dalmations	Mr Torte

Index of Contributors

Sharon Mail was born in Glasgow in 1953. She obtained a BA in Business Studies from Strathclyde University in 1986 and joined Scottish Mutual Assurance, which became part of the Abbey National group, where she worked for 19 years.

In January 2006, Sharon became a full-time journalist working for the Jewish Telegraph Group of Newspapers and now writes freelance. In 2008 she won the Writers' Summer School Diamond Anniversary Article Competition. She is a former Public Relations Officer of the Scottish Association of Writers and has run several writing workshops and courses.